GRAVITY AND LEVITY

Alan McGlashan

Gravity
and
Levity

Houghton Mifflin Company

BOSTON

1976

First American Edition
Copyright © 1976 by Alan McGlashan

Library of Congress Cataloging in Publication Data

McGlashan, Alan.
    Gravity and levity.

    Includes bibliographical references.
    1. Physics — Philosophy.   2. Paradox.
I. Title.
QC6.M317   1976   110   76-22417
ISBN 0-395-24762-4

Printed in the United States of America

c 10 9 8 7 6 5 4 3 2 1

For my two Robins

'One aim of the physical sciences has been to give an exact picture of the material world. One achievement of physics in the 20th century has been to prove that this is impossible . . . There is no absolute knowledge. And those who claim it, whether they are scientists or dogmatists, open the door to tragedy.'

J. BRONOWSKI

July 1973

Contents

Introduction

Science today is in the awkward position of a young woman who has inadvertently become pregnant and wonders how long she can continue in her job. She realises that so far nothing has been noticed, everybody being far too preoccupied with their own affairs. But she also knows that something has happened which is bound very soon to transform the world she lives in.

What has happened is this. Western science since the time of Bacon has been built up on the basis of logic and the causal principle. Generations of scientists have followed this principle with unswerving honesty and dazzling success. Now, while still staunchly true to the logical-causal principle, they find themselves, as a result of the increasing precision of their observations, compelled to make authoritative statements that are logically ridiculous. More disturbing still, current research is forcing upon them the general conclusion that at the most refined and rigorous level of sub-atomic investigation *paradox* is the only form of scientific statement that will fit the facts.

To their credit scientists have not evaded this awkward situation. But they are visibly embarrassed by it. When leading physicists publicly use terms like 'strangeness quantum numbers', describe fluids that are so volatile they can 'pass through a hole that does not exist', and speak of 'forbidden radiation', 'charmed particles' and 'absolute elsewhere'; when they confess to having invented the notion of 'the quark' (surely a misprint for

9

The Snark?) and to be arguing briskly among themselves whether there are four or only three variations of this non-existing particle — they simply cannot conceal their well-bred dismay at finding themselves suddenly involved in these provoking paradoxes. This sort of thing, of course, has happened before. In the 6th century B.C. Pythagoras, first and perhaps greatest polymath in history, who discovered, among many other things, that numbers have a visual form (1 is a point, 2 is a line, 3 a triangle, etc.), found to his dismay that certain numbers, such as the square root of 2, could not be represented in any visual form. He called these numbers arrhetos, 'the unspeakable numbers', and put his followers on oath never to mention their existence.

Contemporary science has behaved better than that. But why should there be *any* dismay? After all, science is not alone in this predicament. When inquiry in any field whatever of human existence reaches a certain depth we are likely to find ourselves in the region of paradox, where every path is strewn with booby-traps for logical minds. By common consent this region has always been declared out of bounds to 'serious' thinkers, and anyone who ventured into it has been dismissed as a mere entertainer. An Aristophanes or a Bernard Shaw could be licensed to amuse us for an hour of an evening; but we all knew, of course, that it was only their fun. The trouble with the recent discoveries by Nobel Prize physicists is that it is impossible to regard them as entertainers.

Yet there they stand, the ultimate Authorities of our time, telling us with an embarrassed air which makes it all the more convincing that scientific inquiry has suddenly broken through into an Alice-in-Wonderland world where every fact is Janus-faced, and reality itself is paradoxical. Their discomfiture is due to the fact that they have no philosophy to offer which can contain their own discoveries. They feel bound in honesty to tell us what they have found, but plainly hope we won't take too much notice of it. Above all, they hope we won't start letting it affect our attitude to everyday life.

In this, at least they are backing a winner. Everyman carries on much as before, and his basic assumptions remain blissfully undisturbed. He is content to leave what he calls 'the egg-heads' to get on with their bizarre activities, which he considers totally irrelevant to his own factual daily life. But the truth is that Everyman has been affected more than he knows, and is in fact reacting everywhere, blindly and dangerously — dangerously because blindly — to the impact of this tremendous and liberating revolution of thought.

Liberating it certainly is. Our generation has been given a heaven-sent chance to cock a snook of jumbo dimensions at all the pedantic father-figures of our school-days — the close-packed circle of severe, unrelenting faces that *knew all the answers*. To burst a paper-bag behind them and watch them jump is the most intoxicating fun, as youth all over the world is finding out. Though youth is often totally vague as to why it is doing this, and what is happening. And not youth only: science itself is still punch-drunk from its own discovery.

The current conflicts of youth against age and authority are in essence a revolt against *smugness*, against the closed, superior attitude of mind which assumes that somewhere there is always a final truth to be found, if only reason is followed patiently to its conclusion. Youth in some unconscious or intuitive way has tuned in to the physicists' discovery that there is no final truth to be found anywhere, that reality in the last resort is ambiguous, open-ended, a recurring balance of contraries;

and with the eager receptiveness of adolescence they have at once embodied it in their crazy-seeming life-style.

Which side each of us is on in this revolt is by no means a matter of chronological age or a way-out ward-robe. The division lies between those who welcome, consciously or purely intuitively, the paradoxical nature of reality, and those who do not. If a man has never asked himself this question he might be in some doubt how to answer. Fortunately there is a simple test. Those of us who welcome the fact find that all attitudes, religious, philosophical or scientific that are devoid of paradox, however, enlightened they may otherwise be, *make us feel uncomfortable*. For us such attitudes point to a universe that does not exist, and which would be boring if it did exist. The longing for a shining future when all doubts and ambiguities will be swept away, the nostalgia for a golden past when no doubts or ambiguities had yet arisen, are equally pathetic fallacies. Our andro-gynous ancestor Adam-Eve tried that second kind of life, and became insufferably bored with the endless delights of Eden — exasperated, in fact, to the point of making the primal adolescent rebellion against all-wise father-figures. Life without choice is intolerable except in early childhood.

This book presents paradox, not as an entertainer's parlour trick, but as a central fact of existence to be trusted and enjoyed. It attempts to transform an uncosy, discomfited reaction to contemporary revelations of the paradoxical world we live in, into a joyous sense that reality could not be other than paradoxical, and that only fools would wish it otherwise. It suggests that from the moment of the awakening of logic in the human mind man has spent his finest energies trying to discover a final truth, which would strangle him if he found it.

INTRODUCTION

The scientific facts collected in this book are nothing new. All it brings forward in this field is old hat to the experts. What is new is the assertion that if ordinary human beings everywhere open their minds and imaginations to the practical implications of what has already been discovered in the esoteric field of micro-physics, they may find they have suddenly brought back laughter and sanity to a sick world. For there is this to be said for the paradoxical attitude that contemporary science has now made philosophically tenable: it scares the pants off the pompous. Pomposity cannot breathe the air of paradox.

I

'Le Coup de Vide'

How deep-rooted an urge is this passion that has possessed so many men throughout history to find a single, unequivocal answer to their enquiries! Particularly scientists — at least till very recently. As Bronowski has said of Einstein: 'Like Newton, and all scientific thinkers, Einstein was in a deep sense a unitarian.' Religious-minded people also tend to seek, behind their varying formulations, a single Creator. But indeed anyone in any branch of human activity who comes up with what even remotely looks like a Final Answer — such as Freud's sexuality theory, or Nietzsche's concept of the Superman — is sure of a world-wide audience of partisans and enemies.

Hidden beneath this time-honoured search for unity lies an element of fear. In spite of what John Keats asserted, men everywhere have a horror of 'uncertainty and doubt.' It is as if an empty abyss were opening beneath their feet, awakening in them that panic reaction that French mountain climbers call *'le coup de vide'*. Frantically searching with fingers and toes for a firm hold on the slippery rock-face of truth, 'Rock of Ages,' we cry, 'cleft for me, Let me hide myself in Thee!'

Our panic misleads us. The abyss below is not the huge Void of outer space, through which we imagine ourselves plunging down, arms outflung, eyes shut, mouth rounded in a soundless scream . . . Instead, a bewildering surprise awaits us. When finally we slip, scrabbling, off the vertiginous rock-face, what gently receives us is — salt water, the sea, *mare* the mother of all life. With a gulp of amazement we find that we can relax and float. Opening our eyes at last we see a ship on the water close beside us, white sails spread for distant adventure; and willing hands to lift us aboard . . . Life offers no greater experience than this surrender of the panic-stricken search for certainty. It is death. And re-birth.

The classic reaction towards uncertainty was perfectly illustrated one summer's day when I was walking by the ornamental lake in Regents Park. A man in a rowing boat caught a crab and fell into the water. Arms and legs wildly flailing, he screamed — 'Help, help! I can't swim!' Finally a bystander shouted back, 'Stand up, you bloody fool!' The drowning man did so — and found that the water just came up to his waist.

But we should not underestimate the benefits that have come to men through this curiously stubborn conviction that there is in the final resort a *single* explanation for the cosmos. It has been the motivating force of many of the greatest human achievements. Pythagoras, as we have seen, reached his miraculous discovery of the relation between music and mathematics only because he was inspired by the over-simplified belief that 'all things are numbers'. Copernicus, who made the world accept that 'the Sun does not go round the Earth, but the Earth goes round the Sun', arrived at his revolutionary idea through his conviction that 'thirty four circles suffice to explain the entire structure of the universe and the entire ballet of the planets.' (It is true that he found himself compelled soon after to add another fourteen circles, and in later life became increasingly doubtful about the whole thing; but the simplistic background of his immensely valuable life-work remained — and was totally mistaken.) It was again this 'certainty' of a unitary explanation of reality that sustained Newton, and enabled him to construct his majestic pattern of the universe, based though it was on his fallacious assumption of the 'absolute reality' of Space and Time.

Even today, when leading scientists and thinkers are at last beginning to catch sight of the paradoxical nature of reality, there is this flourishing French school of structural philosophy, headed by such distinguished figures as Levi-Strauss, Foucault and Lacan, which carries the quest for a single and final explanation of everything to a point which approaches the psychotic. *Structuralism* claims to have already revealed 'the few primary hidden codes' that determine all human thought and behaviour, and is now seeking the master-code behind all codes, 'the system', to use Foucault's words, 'underlying all systems.'

When they find it, that, we must all agree, will be the day.

This tireless quest for the Ultimate Explanation, time after time proved mistaken, survives every exposure, springing up in new forms with each new generation of men. To challenge it is a bold, a Promethean gesture, inviting a Promethean fate. For be sure that the D.F.F.A., Defenders of the Faith in a Final Answer, will not surrender tamely. Their counter-attacks will be the tactics of desperate men. They will fight us on the beaches, they will fight us in the hills, they will never give in.

And in a way they are justified in this implacable reaction. What we are proposing to tamper with — in their view like a child fiddling with the switches of an atomic pile — is the motivation of a large part of all human achievements. We are undermining the moral conviction that a solution can be found for all problems if only we strive for it with resolution and persistence. Take away this conviction, they say, and the human race will become a vast, amorphous mob of "drop-outs." A terrifying prospect. 'Man the barricades!' cry the D.F.F.A.

They could be right. It is possible that men will lose

all heart in the struggle for existence unless they are sustained by the hope of reaching a millenium, however distant, and a final answer to all their afflictions. It may be that a human being is kept going only by the kind of faith that apparently supports the coral insect: a creature that lives and toils and dies in the dark of the sea, in the obscure foreknowledge that out of the skeletons of a billion generations of its kind there will one day rise up from the tropical ocean a white and shining Coral Island. It must after all be a similar conviction that sustains the military mind in its belief that, built on the dead bodies of millions of men, women and children, there will one day rise the glorious white temple of Victory. Constructed, like a coral island, of skeletons.

It is possible that man will collapse without such dubious inventives. But I do not believe it. We have been bedevilled for centuries by the vision of Nature as a marvellously balanced and coordinated system — which it is — moving with a precision and harmony of parts that imply an underlying unitary structure — if only we could see it. Our failure to grasp unity behind apparent diversity, lies, we are taught, in our own uncertain selves. It is because *we* are such divided, conflict-ridden creatures that the grand, simple, unitary nature of Reality is still hidden from us. 'The fault lies in ourselves,' we are assured, alike by poet and preacher.

What if the truth were otherwise? What if it were Reality that is always and everywhere ambiguous, paradoxical, open-ended? Such an insight at once lifts from us part of 'the burden of the mystery', without lessening the mystery. And it transfers on the instant a multitude of doubts and dilemmas from the heart of man to the heart of Reality. If these two things can be accomplished without sacrifice of intellectual honesty they are surely worth doing. But this way of looking at Reality does more. Its unique reward is to allow a man — paradoxically — to be single-minded in his activities because he knows that Reality is not so.

A statement like that requires amplification. To be single-minded is immensely difficult. So much so that single-mindedness in any activity, even an absurd or an evil one, rouses in most of us at least a grudging admiration. Few would think it worth while to squat night and day for thirty-three years on the top of a sixty foot pillar. Yet, in spite of its absurdity, and even after the psycho-analysts have had their say about him, something in us whispers, 'Damn it, the man must have had *guts.*' And we give expression to this feeling by continuing to remember the name and occupation of St. Simeon Stylites for more than fifteen hundred years.

We are unanimous, nevertheless, in considering his single-mindedness to have been ludicrously ill-directed. And here lies the core of the matter. To be totally committed in any direction carries inescapably the corroding anxiety that one may have made the wrong choice, nailed one's colours to a broken mast, sacrificed one's whole life to an empty dream. Even the deeply religious person can only cry: 'Lord, I believe; help Thou mine unbelief.' In a moment of self-doubt even so great a poet as John Keats confided to his friend Bailey, 'I am sometimes so very sceptical as to think Poetry itself a mere Jack o' Lantern to amuse whoever may chance to be struck by its brilliance.' H.G. Wells went further: 'A committed writer is not a man; he is a mere footnote to reality.' Doubt is the canker at the heart of all human belief. If an individual is lucky enough, and simple enough, to have no shadow of doubt about the rightness of his beliefs others will do his doubting for him.

But if Reality were once seen, as contemporary science is beginning to prove, as itself resting on paradox, itself an endlessly elusive balance of contraries, a man would then be free to commit himself totally, without anxiety, to whatever reveals itself as truth to him. There would be no lurking fear that perhaps his whole approach to life had been mistaken. From the start he would recognise with perfect good humour that no effort of his could ever lead to a final, unassailable truth; it could lead only to the establishment of a worthy opposition to whatever might be advanced against it. Dogmatism would be out of fashion. It would be seen as the pretentious error it is. This, it will be said, is the recognised creed of every scientist. But you have only to listen to the abuse, lobbying and back-biting aroused at any Congress of scientists to realise that they don't believe a word of it.

When I was a child, mice, which were always to be found in the basement kitchens of those days, were caught in wire traps set every night on the kitchen floor. In the morning I would see the luckless mouse caught securely in the wire cage. But I noticed that he always managed to push his long tail through the wire mesh, and it would be wriggling wildly in the free air. For me, truth is that mouse. When we think we have caught it, there is always the defiant tail left outside of the most ingenious cage we can devise.

In any case it is not enough to offer an intellectual acceptance of the proposition that truth dances for ever just out of reach of any possible formulation. What is needed is to *delight* in this fact, to see in it a guarantee that the world is open-ended, inexhaustibly rich in meaning, and eternally resistant to Messianic solutions. What is needed is to relax and to begin to look on ultimate questions not as problems to be solved, but as mysteries that save us from despair. 'Life is not a series of problems', said the French philosopher Gabriel Marcel, 'it is a network of mysteries'.

The desire to transcend all polarities and reach unity is a tragic human error. Certainly we should practise to pass beyond the grosser polarities and become aware of, and be conditioned by, more and more subtle opposites. But as to the unity that lies beyond, we must while we live, as Simone Weil suggests, learn 'to adore the distance' between ourselves and what we seek. It is the error, the sublime error, of mystics to see their 'moment of illumination' as an *absolute,* beyond all opposites. For such a moment to exist at all, its opposite, a nadir of total, meaningless emptiness, must also exist. The reward of dying, it may be, is to pass through a gateway into that unimaginable region where all opposites meet and melt.

Questions, of course, are a challenge to human ingenuity, and are there to be answered one after another to the best of human ability — till we reach the ultimate questions that are concerned with the irreducible polarities of life and death, time and eternity, beginnings and endings. Man started asking these questions a long, long time ago, and is no nearer the answers now than he was then. Already, at the dawn of Indian civilisation, the tenth hymn of the Rig Veda is hammering away at the locked doors of the ultimate:

Being, then was not, nor not-being.
The air was not, nor the sky above it.
What kept closing in? Where?
And whose the enclosure?
Was the plunging abyss all water?
Who knows it, and who shall declare
Where this Creation was born, and whence it came?

Who indeed? At this point we should start to make daisy-chains of question-marks. They are, as it happens, conveniently looped for the purpose.

2

Loosening-up

A simple way of arriving at recognition of the nature of all human experiencing is to consider the many fields in which a series begins logically, factually, measurably, and ends in a mocking question-mark. What, for instance, could be more definite and down-to-earth than milli-metre, centimetre, metre, kilometre? But extend this series to the measurement of inter-galactic distances and to the limits of the cosmos, and you are at once faced with unanswerable problems, and involved in abstruse theories about the curvature of Space. At this level your careful measurements start wriggling about like epileptic snakes.

The same thing happens to minutes, hours, days and years, which begin rationally enough and end facing the ultimate mystery of Time. Speed, too, starting with metres per minute and ending in the wild-eyed fantasy of galaxies of stars receding at ever-increasing speed till they surpass the speed of light, at which point they are said to cease to exist. Moreover all these and many other series are open-ended in *both* directions. Extend any of them in the direction of the infinitely small instead of the infinitely large, and you find yourself in the equally irrational and crazy world of micro-physics, where un-predictability is the only thing that is predictable.

Paradox, in fact, is not an intellectual parlour-trick; it is the Rule by which we live, the existential situation of man, the basis of human consciousness. It is also the guarantee that Reality will remain for ever the dawn-fresh, tantalising prize that men will reach for but never, luckily for them, possess.

Many men have always known this. Plato understood it when he spoke of that 'Something about which we can know only that it exists, and that nothing else can ever be desired, except in error.' St. Augustine, himself a highly paradoxical personality, saw the beauty and necessity of paradox: 'As speech', he once said, 'is enriched by antitheses, so the beauty of the course of this world is achieved by the opposition of contraries arranged, as it were, by an eloquence not of words but of things.' Nearer to our own day, A.N. Whitehead defined religion in terms which make it a perfect example of a paradoxical quest. 'Religion', he says, 'is the vision of something which stands beyond, behind and within the passing flux of immediate things; something which is real, yet waiting to be realised; something which is a remote possibility, yet the greatest of all present facts; something that gives meaning to all that passes, yet eludes comprehension; something whose possession is the final good, yet is beyond all reach; something which is the ultimate ideal, and the hopeless quest.'

These being the views of three not inconsiderable figures — a philosopher, a saint and a scientist — it would seem that paradox as a central fact of human existence has its serious supporters.

We are altogether too complacent, too rigid in our conclusions about life. Carlos Castanada speaks of 'The dogmatic certainty, which we all share, that the validity of our perceptions, or our reality of the world, is not to be questioned.' We sit back, like T.S. Eliot's commuter, 'assured of certain certainties' that are not certainties at all. Clever as the human being may be, there are a surprising number of things he has forgotten how to do. He has forgotten, for instance, how to digest food without a stomach, how to breathe without lungs, how to excrete uric acid without kidneys and expel it without a bladder. He has even forgotten how to make movements without muscles. Yet, as J.W. Kratch reminds us, there are living creatures called protozoans in every part of the world at this moment who are doing all these things. Protozoans are, of course, simple souls, being composed of a single cell. But higher up the evolutionary scale there are many other creatures daily performing what is humanly impossible. There is, for instance, that curious fish the Gymnarchus which although blind contrives to 'see' by self-generated electronic messages, successfully pursuing and capturing by this means the darting, twisting small fish on which it feeds; and the homely honey-bee whose dancing discloses a wealth and precision of meaning that no human choreographer can match. There is the tern, which performs the unbelievable muscular feat of flying from the Arctic to the Antarctic and back some thirty times in the course of its life. These literally superhuman feats, however, are easily outclassed by a small coelenterate called the Hydra. If you cut off a Hydra's head it will grow a new one.

Even in the sphere of knowledge, that proudest of human achievements, there are areas in which our awareness cannot compare with that of some of our very humblest neighbours on the earth. There are rhythms in nature, particularly solar and lunar rhythms, to which we are grossly insensitive in contrast to many other forms of life. A large body of evidence, which is increasing almost daily, suggests that many living things have an awareness of the changing phases of the sun and moon, and a finely adjusted response to the electro-magnetic influences proceeding from them, which is far beyond human powers; or at least far beyond any attention we have yet given to these matters. It may for instance come as a surprise to some people to learn that 'potatoes, algae, carrots, earthworms, and salamanders all "know" where the moon is, whether it has just appeared over the horizon, whether it is at the zenith, or whether it is seting,' and respond to the knowledge by an appropriate adjustment of their metabolism. To be outclassed in any branch of knowledge by a potato should surely loosen up the most arrogant intellectual.

The possibility arises that there could be some form of mind or mental processes without brain. Plants have neither brain nor nerve-tissue, yet the cells of the Venus plant are capable of the instantaneous, concerted, purposive action — equivalent to a tiger-spring — required to entice and then suddenly capture a passing fly. (Incidentally, without either mouth or stomach the fly-catching plant is able to eat and digest the fly, probably with a good deal of quiet enjoyment.) An American researcher, Cleve Backster, has achieved world-wide attention by his claim to have demonstrated that plants are actually sensitive to emotional stress. His results appear to have been confirmed by controlled tests in several separate research laboratories, and are moreover in line with the long-published researches of Chandra Bose the distinguished Indian scientist; though it is hardly necessary to add that these results have been scornfully dismissed by indignant members of the Door-Slammers' Union. The activities of this ancient and powerful Union will be discussed in the next chapter.

However, it may be with the daring hypothesis of emotionality in plants, all the other statements above are established beyond reasonable doubt. Simply to ignore them can lead to an irritating anthropomorphism. In the light of them what becomes, for example, of the dismissive assertions that there can be no mental life on any of the planets comparable with human mental life, unless the planets' atmosphere and conditions can support forms of life with brain-boxes as large as our own? These people are not giving nearly enough credit to the *ingenuity* of the life-force. They could be right that on other planets there is no life comparable to that of human beings — but not for the kind of reasons they put forward. They should loosen up.

Logical minds that find it difficult or distateful to loosen up in this way would do well to read a highly ingenious essay, first published in 1971, on the subject of *The Equivocal Universe*. The authors' demonstration of the open-ended nature of the universe is, for the logically-minded, disarmingly objective. Very briefly, their argument consists in drawing our attention once more to an image which has intrigued us all since childhood, the image of the Chalice and the two Faces:

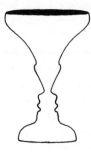

They point out that two important facts emerge as we look at this image. In the authors' own words —

'(1) *We cannot see the Chalice and the Faces simultaneously.* However rapidly we may oscillate between the chalice and the faces, we cannot see both interpretations at once. If we *could* do that, we should see nothing, a void; both chalice and faces would vanish.

(2) *The status of both interpretations is the same.* We cannot say that the chalice is the true interpretation

and the faces false, nor that the faces are true and the chalice false.'

The authors then work out with clarity and humour the implications of these two equivocal facts in relation to the way in which we normally see the world. The implications are considerable. 'It may be', they suggest, 'that the two worlds we live in, physical and meta-physical, material and anti-material, exist in a relation-ship analogous to that of the chalice and the faces: we can only see one at a time, each filters out the other.' Since we have been taught by both science and religion to search beyond all apparent dualities for a single inter-pretation of the world, and since this unity of inter-pretation is 'equated in our minds with logical consis-tency, and is held up to us as a virtue synonymous with honesty and integrity', then the scene is set for endless sterile conflict. On every basic issue, say these authors, men will find themselves separated into two opposing groups, the 'Chalice-landers' and the 'Face-landers', each entrenched in their own equally valid world, eyeing the opposition with unappeasable alarm and distrust.

The point has been made before. At the turn of the 19th century Gilbert and Sullivan were saying much the same thing in expressing their amused surprise that — in their simpler political day —

Every little Englishman that's born into this world alive Is either a little Liberal or, else a little Conservative.

Ridiculous as it seems for adults to play these endless games of Oranges and Lemons, it must be remembered that the clash of opinions is a time-honoured way of testing their validity. 'Without contraries, no progress', said William Blake. Once we can accept that the human mind is so constructed that only by taking sides can it get to grips with many of its problems, we are free to conceive and sometimes to enter that region of our psyche from which these furious battles are seen to be nothing more than necessities of our mental mechanism; shadow-fights where victory of either side only provides the stimulus for further conflict.

Even if we achieve this degree of self-awareness, the furious battles will of course continue. But less viciously perhaps, less rancorously, with less commitment to the monstrous illusion of total victory. They will continue because there is a spark of spiritual jingoism in the human psyche which seems to be inextinguishable. Students everywhere will mount one kind of war as a protest against another kind of war. Even so fine a spirit as Blake can shout —

> We shall not cease from mental strife,
> Nor shall the sword sleep in our hand
> Till we have built Jerusalem —.

It all sounds splendidly heroic, but flashing swords do not lead to the building of Jerusalem, but to the building of long, long graveyards filled with identical little wooden crosses.

There is a part of our psyche which already knows this; but we don't live there. We don't live there because of the terrifying Condition of Entry: to accept gladly in ourselves a state of 'uncertainty and doubt' that is beyond all human effort or appeal. We shudder away from the freedoms this would create, not daring to give up the hope of one day finding unity and a final answer.

Why on earth is the human mind so hell-bent on finding unity? Suppose we did suddenly arrive at the final, unitary, incontrovertible truth as to the nature of Reality — that mirage which we have passionately pursued for all these centuries. What a strait-jacket it would prove to be! Man would have robbed himself of choice.

For once such an ultimate truth were universally believed, failure to accept it would simply prove a man to be an enemy of society, or mentally deranged. On either count he would be liable to find himself locked up. The 'goodies' and the 'baddies' would be branded instantly and automatically by a gross over-simplification reminiscent of a Calvinist vision of the Last Judgement, or even more, of the technique of government in a modern totalitarian state: a night-mare world where freedom, not merely of action but of thought, would be in eternal exile. Precisely the kind of choice-deprived world which our prime ancestor, Adam-Eve, found intolerable.

And if, like him, we found ourselves trapped in so claustrophobic a universe, we should be driven, as he was, to commit some huge, iconoclastic crime to earn once more our banishment beyond the stifling gates of Paradise.

3

Blind Man's Bluff

You might suppose that the idea of the world being open-ended, translucent, pointing beyond itself, would be attractive to almost everyone, but this is by no means so. A very large number of people cannot rest until they have 'proved' the opposite. Many eminent figures, past and present, are paid-up, card-carrying members of the powerful trade union of Door-Slammers and Full-Stoppers, whose banner bears the strange device: 'Stop the World, we want to get off!'

It is a kind of collective agoraphobia. Such people cannot feel cosy in an open-ended world, so they have to bustle about closing doors and locking windows in the human mind, setting burglar alarms and nailing 'Beware of the Dog!' to the gate — before they can settle down to their night's rest, or their day's work. Keats in one of his Letters pin-points the type perfectly in describing his friend Dilke as a man 'who cannot feel he has a personal identity unless he has made up his mind about everything.' And Keats adds: 'The only means of strengthening one's intellect is to make up one's mind about nothing — to let the mind be a thoroughfare for all thoughts, not a select party.' This, of course, is heresy to the Door-Slammers Union.

The list of past presidents of the Union is impressive. There is, for instance, the famous French chemist Berthelot, who qualifies as an early president with his pronouncement, in 1887, 'From now on there is no mystery about the Universe.' A truly cosmic Door-Slam, which should have put the Universe permanently in its place. (Half a century later, however, we find Professor J.B. Haldane murmuring, 'The universe may be not only queerer than we suppose, but queerer than we *can* suppose.')

1895 was a bumper year for the Union, in which there were a number of contenders for the presidential chair. Lord Kelvin started favourite that year, by announcing with all the authority of a reigning President of the Royal Society: 'Heavier-than-air flying machines are impossible.' The bearded Victorian rank and file of the Union probably gave him a standing ovation for this comforting assurance. Running him close came Mons. Brunetiere, who officially proclaimed 'the bankruptcy of Science.' At the same time Professor Lippmann told one of his pupils that 'physics is a subject that is exhausted . . . and you had better turn your attention to something else.' (The pupil's name was Heilbronner, who became a famous modern physicist.)

That was a vintage year. But even today competition for the presidency is almost as keen. Contemporary aspirants would have to include that ambiguous figure Pere Teilhard de Chardin, who could be raised posthumously to the status of Union president after the manner in which the Catholic Church honours its departed saints. To cite Pere Teilhard in this connection may seem shocking to some. As a theologian and mystic — though frowned on by the Catholic Church of which he was a priest — he possessed undeniable spiritual greatness. It was precisely this which gave weight to his curious blind spots as a philosopher. Heredity may have played a part. On his father's side he was descended from Voltaire, on his mother's from Pascal; and it could be that the inner discord created by this paradoxical inheritance was the cause of his overwhelming need to reach unity and finality. Be that as it may, Pere Teilhard clearly deserves to be considered as a presidential candidate, in view of his Full-Stop declaration on the theory of evolution. 'Like all things in the universe,' said Teilhard, 'life is and can only be a "size" of evolutionary nature and dimensions . . . . This is the fundamental fact' (not even *a* fundamental fact, note, but *the* fundamental fact) 'and . . . *the evidence for it is henceforward above all verification, as well as being immune from any subsequent contradiction by experience.*' Alas for the sanguine hopes of Full-Stoppers. Nothing in heaven or earth is quite as certain as all that.

The structuralist leader Foucault, whom we have already observed searching for the Ultimate Code that governs human behaviour, could also be considered; but the final vote must surely go to Professor Jacques Monod of the Institut Pasteur. In his book *Chance and Necessity* he has this to say about chance-mutation: 'Chance alone is at the source of every innovation, of all creation in the biosphere . . . This central concept of modern biology is no longer one among other possible or even conceivable hypotheses. It is today the *sole* conceivable hypothesis, the only one that squares with observed and tested fact. And nothing warrants the supposition – or the hope – that on this score our position is ever likely to be revised.'

It is immaterial what particular assertion a Full-Stopper happens to make. The point lies in the *quality* of the assertion. Although in the two last examples I have given, Pere Teilhard and Professor Monod are maintaining precisely opposite opinions – Design as a final evolutionary truth as against Chance – they are brothers under the skin, recognisable members of the Union, not only in the brutal arrogance of their assertions but also in the curious similarity of their language.

32

To be able to spot this style instantly, irrespective of what it is asserting, and of the impressive qualifications of the asserter, is essential if the world is to be kept, as it again has a chance to be, alive and open-ended. It is time to put a stop to this centuries-old game of Blind Man's Bluff, in which the eminence of the Blind Man gives world-wide currency to his obstructive bluff. From hindsight these distinguished obstructionists look foolish enough; but in their own generation they succeed in closing many a door for many a day. In itself this is of no great significance — if we choose to forget that behind most of these closed doors lies a defeated and heart-broken genius — since all such doors tend to re-open, irresistibly, in time. But the underlying aim of the Door-Slammers should never be lost sight of. It could succeed, and it is infinitely sinister: to create a climate of opinion in which it would be universally accepted that although there are goals still to be reached, the premises underlying the method of approach to these goals have been laid down once and for all and are never again to be open to question. In the Monod-Teilhard language, they are 'the sole conceivable hypotheses' and 'henceforward beyond all verification as well as being immune from any subsequent contradiction.'

This bull-necked refusal to grant even the elementary rights of co-existence to an opposing idea reaches its peak performance in the hardly believable outburst of the world-famous physicist Heinrich Helmholtz on the subject of telepathy: 'Neither the testimony of all the Fellows of the Royal Society', cries the bold Helmholtz, 'nor even the evidence of my own senses, would lead me to believe in the transmission of thought from one person to another independently of the recognised channels of sense.' For an eminent scientist to start shouting, 'I

33

won't believe it, even if it's *proved* true!' is a trifle embarrassing.

Nevertheless it carries weight. The obstructive power of a leader of the Door-Slammers' Union — who is always an expert at Blind Man's Bluff — should not be underestimated, whether in religion or science. Countless illustrations of this fact are available, but three are enough. All the world knows of the Papal pressure that forced Galileo to recant his "false and heretical" opinion that the earth was *not* stationary, and *not* the centre of the Universe. Two hundred years later the chemical manufacture of industrial diamonds was delayed for decades because 'a chemist of genius, a Mons. Moissan, was forced to recant and declare in public that he had not manufactured diamonds but had made a mistake in an experiment.' In 1924 a brilliant Austrian biologist, Dr. Paul Kammerer, committed suicide, having been 'discredited' as a scientist by what was possibly the most outrageous piece of academic skulduggery on record. The full story can be read in Arthus Koestler's fascinating book *The Case of the Midwife Toad*.

Neither Galileo, Moissan nor Paul Kammerer recanted in their hearts. They were simply three losers in the vicious game of Blind Man's Bluff.

Very occasionally a brave, unquenchable spirit arises who can stand up to the Blind Men, and call their magisterial bluff. Chandra Bose, a highly unorthodox scientist living in Calcutta at the turn of the present century, survived half a lifetime of ridicule, near-slander and contempt to end his days as Sir Jagadis Chandra Bose, F.R.S. It could be said, however, that he had merely been kicked upstairs by the scientific Establishment, since his central and revolutionary discovery — that all things in the universe, inanimate as well as animate, are pulsing with life and responsiveness — was almost totally ignored for the next 70 years. Only now, in the para-doxical climate of contemporary physics, is this dis-covery beginning to be recognised as the all-transform-ing intuition of a scientific genius.

Pride and Prejudice are the hidden human factors moti-vating most of these eminent obstructionists. But a more sinister factor, the profit-motive, is operative in certain cases. At this moment the thin covering of soil which makes our planet habitable is faced with catastrophic yet avoidable risks on this account. Rachel Carson in America with *Silent Spring*, in England McCarrison's *Nutrition and National Health* and Howard's *The Soil and Health*, to mention only a scatter of names, have been shouting at us for the last 30 years that the land is being poisoned and de-natured by the tens of millions of tons of artificial fertilisers and chemical pesticides that are poured upon it year after year. And through the devitalised soil, the plants that grow on it, the animals that eat the plants, and finally the human beings who eat the animals, are being progressively devitalised in their turn.

Books have been written, lectures delivered, practical examples shown of enlightened farmers more than doubling their crops without chemical aid . . . all without effect. Farmers in the main go on de-naturing their precious soil. Ears have they and hear not. Eyes have they and see not. The reason? Inertia, plus a con-tinuous bombardment by counter-arguments. Authors of the counter-arguments? The farming-chemicals industry is now very Big Business indeed. These par-ticular Blind Men can see in one direction with remark-able clarity — and what they see is an increasing sale for their dubious wares in Western countries, and an illimi-tably expanding market in the developing countries throughout the world. Where there is this kind of vision, the people perish.

35

4

Concerning Humbug

The previous chapter may sound like a wholesale accu-
sation of bad faith against certain eminent custodians of
science and religion. It is nothing of the sort. With rare
exceptions (of which the Kammerer tragedy may be
one) these authoritative voices are declaring what they
honestly, even passionately, believe to be true. To see
them in the role of 'baddies' deliberately trying to crush
the intuitions of virtuous and lonely genius is to mis-
read the whole situation, which is a far more interesting
one.

Plainly it is useful for a man to know if and when he
is being humbugged by expert opinion. This holds for
every field of knowledge, but in none is it more vital to
us than in matters of health. To examine the possibility
of humbug in medicine is surely worth everyone's attention. It also throws light on the wider question of good
and bad faith among experts of all kinds.

When you begin to look into it, medical humbug is a
surprisingly complex subject. The idea that there is on
the one hand a shining body of proven scientific
remedies, and on the other a dark mass of ignorant
superstitions and old wives' tales, is very wide of the
mark. Humbug has always flourished as luxuriantly
inside the medical profession as outside it.

It depends, of course, on what you mean by 'humbug'. There is a sense in which it would be equally true
to say that there is practically no humbug about healing
whether inside or outside the profession. The dictionary

(OED) says that the word 'humbug' means 'fraud, deception, imposture', and in this strict sense there is not, nor has there ever been much humbug in the art of healing. The advocates of techniques that now seem to us totally absurd — such as, for instance, the drinking of a decoction of the soles of old shoes as a cure for dysentery — have always had a powerful if pathetic conviction of the efficacy of their remedies. They may have been self-deceivers, but were seldom deliberate deceivers of others. Their rivals and enemies of course called them 'quacks' and 'charlatans', but this was largely inspired by jealousy of their success with the public. It is in fact very difficult to cure anybody of anything by means of a remedy in which you yourself have no faith. The successful doctor, no less than the successful 'quack' is the man who is really convinced he has got something.

Every medical man has had experiences of achieving impressive results with a certain drug, *so long as he believed in it himself*. As soon as he has some failures and begins to doubt its remedial powers, the results on patients tail off, and in a few months the 'wonder-drug' is, as far as that practitioner is concerned, discarded and forgotten.

This is, after all, not surprising. Such powerful forces are at work. The sick are so desperately anxious to be well again, the doctors so fired by the possibility of discovering something that will truly alleviate human suffering, that the temptation for the doctor to jump to the conclusion that he has found a new remedy, and for the patient to believe him, is at times irresistible.

Alerted by the new insights of psychology, modern medicine recognises this temptation and tries to minimise it by such measures as 'double-blind control tests'. In these tests neither doctor nor patient knows at the time if the tablet being administered is the new drug, or some harmless inert tablet that looks identical. The trouble about this admirably cautious procedure is that it deliberately throws away one of the most powerful healing forces in human life — the enthusiastic belief of both patient and doctor in the remedy employed. Here is where the so-called quacks and charlatans step in. They have no reservations, wait for no double-blind tests, to proclaim their confidence in themselves and the efficacy of their remedy. This confidence is often transmitted to the patient who promptly recovers. And orthodox medical men have the mortification of watching a man, using a form of treatment which they suspect or even know to be unsound, curing a case where their own orthodox methods have failed.

The question arises: *is this humbug*?

Perhaps it depends on the point of view. The patient himself is apt to declare sturdily, 'I couldn't care less which of you is right. All I know is that since going to Professor Quack, whereas before I was sick, now I am well.'

Belief in the efficacy of your treatment applies not only to drugs, but also, more alarmingly, to surgical operations. It is within the memory of many of us that a child who had several attacks of sore throat would almost automatically have its tonsils and adenoids removed. Statistics and authoritative text-books of the period 'proved' how correct and beneficial this procedure was. Now, when belief in this particular measure has dwindled, statistics and authoritative text-books of today, 'prove' precisely the opposite. This is not due to deliberate manipulation of the statistics. The procedure is no longer believed in; so it no longer works. The thing which was officially approved of by one medical generation is then scornfully condemned by the next.

In making this statement of fact I have no intention

to criticise the profession. This is the way all science must proceed – by trial and error. What is important, however, in order to keep a clear head among the marvels of modern medicine, is to set all contemporary discoveries in the sober light of historical perspective, and to recognise that, especially in the field of human suffering, it is not always statistics that give rise to belief. It has sometimes occurred that belief has unconsciously influenced statistics, giving temporary scientific popularity to what later turns out to be no better than an old wives' tale.

To say this is not to deny or decry the enormous benefits which modern medicine has brought to man. The reduction of infant mortality, the elimination or control of many of what used to be killer diseases, such as tuberculosis, diabetes and pneumonia, and the consequent improved expectation of life – these things are ample proof of the spectacular advance of medical science. (The fact that these same successes have accelerated the greatest of all menaces to the human race – the population explosion – cannot be blamed on medical science, whose sufficient function is to save and heal). But it is a reminder that neither the professional nor the layman should accept too eagerly every advance in medical treatment. Occasionally, as in the thalidomide catastrophe and the current controversy over the contraceptive pill, it may prove to be an advance in a tragic direction.

All the same, medicine has come a long way since its earliest days. The art of healing is perhaps the oldest profession bar one, and has had many exotic practitioners. The first known portrait of a medical man is to be found on a wall of the Grotto of Trois Freres in the Pyrenees. He is completely enclosed in animal skin, and wears antlers and a startled look. This picture was painted in Cro-Magnon times, more than 20,000 years ago.

Down the long corridors of time since then has marched a straggling multi-coloured army of healers: naked witch-doctors in terrifying masks, fur-clad shamans of Siberia, white-robed physicians of classical Greece (in a brief period of medical insight and wisdom inspired by Hippocrates and the legendary Aesculapius); hooded mediaeval figures labouring with furnace and crucible to discover the alchemical 'Elixir of Life'; herbalists, led by the genius of second century Galen, grubbing industriously (as they do to this day) in wood or hedgerow; old crones in city back-streets ready to sell secret remedies of every kind, not excluding abortifacients and love-philtres, or even, at a pinch, poison . . . . The pageant is unending and as colourful as a carnival . . . Out of the early sixteenth century strides the giant figure of Paracelsus, loud, hectoring and obscene — but a genius. He smashes the gentle 1,400-year reign of herbalist Galen, and prescribes new and powerful drugs, such as mercury for syphilis, on the ruthless principle of kill-or-cure. He starts a search for more and more potent and dangerous drugs that has never flagged for four hundred years, and is in fact the dubious mainspring of modern pharmaceutics.

In the seventeenth century, a hundred years after rough-necked Paracelsus, there begins to emerge a new, self-conscious image of the 'eminent physician'. For the first time, medical men become pompous and fashionable. Medical dandies appear, distinguished equally for arrogance and ignorance, mincing for the next 200 years through the royal courts of Europe in their wigs and brocades and, as emblem of their calling, their gold-headed canes. These worthies become the butts of the savage cartoonists of their day, such as Hogarth and Gilroy, who portray them as disputing loftily with each

other — while the patient dies. Their treatments and pre-
scriptions have to be seen to be believed. If ever humbug flourished within the medical profession, it was
then. But again was this humbug in the strict sense, that
is, a deliberate deception of others? It was perhaps the
truth as they saw it?

Yet it is hard to credit that any honest and intelligent
physician in *any* era could believe in the efficacy of
some of the drugs then prescribed — as, for example,
usnea, which was moss scraped from the skull of a mur-
derer who had been hanged in chains. This remarkable
remedy was all the rage in medical circles for a long time
— so long that it was still listed as an official drug in the
British Pharmacopeia in the nineteenth century, and the
first edition of the Encyclopaedia Britannica contains a
learned article on its curative properties. A sick person
in the seventeenth and eighteenth centuries was liable to
be dosed, on the best medical advice, not only with
usnea, but with powdered mummy, the horn of the non-
existent unicorn, liquid gold, crushed bugs, lice and
toads, and the soles of old shoes. Urine was another favourite remedy, as a mouth-wash for toothache and other
minor complaints. One prescription begins: 'For Chapped
Lips. Take a pint of yr owne Watter . . .' In those days it
paid a man to stay healthy.

These being the beliefs and practices of the learned
physicians in the sixteenth, seventeenth and eighteenth
centuries, it might be supposed that the ignorant
country-folk of the same period would have produced
even more fantastic remedies. But not so. There may be
something in country life that keeps a man closer to
Nature — and to sanity. For the most part the old wives
of the countryside relied on simple methods, often herbal remedies almost unaltered since Galen's day, for
the cure of the sick. A great many of their concoctions

were of course completely useless, though seldom actively harmful. But just occasionally they hit on something far in advance of their times. We should not forget the old countrywoman who seemed to be having a great success treating dropsy with an infusion of fox-gloves from her garden. Her fame became nation-wide, to the lofty amusement of the famous physicians of the day. Then it was discovered that her simple infusion contained a hitherto unknown drug called Digitalis, which is still among the most valuable drugs we have. And it is only recently that the mould on oranges, used many years ago by country-folk for infected wounds, was shown to be a source of Penicillin. Old wives some-times knew a thing or two, as I once learned from per-sonal experience.

When I began practice in the country, I was one day called to see an old woman who was crippled by a large varicose ulcer encircling her ankle. My own attempt to cure her was a complete failure, as were the efforts of a specialist I called in for consultation. At this point her still more ancient husband said to me, 'Now you medical men have had a shot at it, will you leave her alone for a couple of weeks, and let me have a try? I think I can cure her.' A fortnight later I came back to find the ulcer completely gone. It took an hour's persuasion to get the old man to reveal his treatment. He had taken a large rhubarb leaf from his allotment, wrapped it, all un-washed as it was, round the ankle, and cured it. With the arrogance of youth I put it down to coincidence and thought no more of it. Now, thirty years later, it would not surprise me if one day soon some brilliant chemist, using the most advanced fractional research technique, succeeds in isolating an ingredient in rhubarb leaves that is specific for the healing of varicose ulcers.

In addition to herbal remedies, non-medical healers

from the earliest times tried to cure the sick in two other ways: by the use of *magic*, or by the power of *faith*. Though related, these two approaches were opposites. Both effected cures through supernatural forces, but *magic* was connected with the dark realm of witches, who were far readier, it was thought, to strike down or even destroy a man than to cure him. For one wise old woman who would cure warts by rubbing them with a raw potato freshly dug out of the ground under a full moon, or make a barren wife fertile by passing her at the stroke of midnight through a rock with a circular hole in it, there were a dozen witches, so it was believed, who would bring down on you ill-health or ill-luck at the drop of a hat. Their supposed misdoings, in fact, brought many of the poor wretches to the stake or the scaffold.

Faith-healing, on the other hand, was entirely beneficent in its effects, and was practised mainly by saints and exceptionally holy persons. Even Royalty deigned to take part in this form of therapy, specialising mainly in the cure of tuberculous glands of the neck, known then as 'the King's Evil', by means of 'the Royal Touch'. Henry VIII also dispensed 'cramp-rings' for the cure of cramps and fits, but this was a side-line. Treatment for 'the King's Evil' began in the time of Edward the Confessor (who, being a saint as well as a King, was reputed to be very good at it), and continued for centuries. An unlikely recipient of this form of treatment was the irascible Dr. Samuel Johnson, who received 'the Royal Touch' from Queen Anne. He was, however, only four years old at the time, so presumably was not consulted.

Saintly persons, though credited with the ability to cure any disease, were mainly employed therapeutically for the casting out of devils from the mentally afflicted. It was emphasized that the saint had to be careful to keep his lips closed at the moment of expulsion, lest the devil should jump out of the patient's mouth into his own.

Witchcraft, black and white, the 'Royal Touch', the 'casting out of devils' — are we back in the realm of medical humbug? It is not easy to decide. As far as the 'Royal Touch' was concerned it is probable that at least some of our Kings performed it with tongue in cheek and regarded it as pure humbug. William III, for example, used to accompany the 'Royal Touch' with the double-edged words, 'May God give you better health, and more sense.'

Witches are now out of favour — though covens do exist to this day in various parts of Great Britain — but in their heyday there is evidence that witches themselves believed strongly in their own magic powers. In other words, they were not guilty of humbug.

In the matter of healing the sick by faith, which is, in 1976, perhaps the most flourishing form of non-medical therapy, the charge of humbug is clearly untenable. Faith-healers of many cults are more numerous today than at any time in the past, and some of them present reasonable claims to recognition, and undeniable successes. Apart from the cults, there is another form of faith-healing, important but unobstrusive and little known. A book published in 1964 (*The Nature of Healing*, written by an anonymous consultant psychiatrist of high standing) offers striking evidence of the presence among us of 'natural healers', who are often not even aware of their gift. The author regards these natural healers as totally distinct from all other kinds of faith-healing. Even the Church, though frowning on the idea of individuals with this power, officially believes in the capacity of priests, as humble instruments of the Divine, to cure the sick by what is called 'charismatic healing'. Finally orthodox medicine has begun reluctantly to accept hypnotism — which depends entirely on the power of faith in a non-religious sense — as a valid form of therapy. It would be a bold materialist who would sweep all these things aside as humbug — though there'are no doubt some who would be happy to do so.

The odd thing is that in spite of the strongly rationalistic bias of our time a certain number of bizarre and ancient remedies are now coming back into vogue, supported of course by current scientific theories. 'Casting out devils', for instance, has a truly mediaeval ring about it, but it would be hard to find a better overall description of the work of a present day psychiatrist. It is perhaps fortunate that he no longer needs to be a saint. Though it could be that the shortage of saints is what is wrong with contemporary psychology.

Swallowing liquid gold seems, again, a purely romantic remedy for disease — yet today it forms the basis, as an injection, for the most recent treatment for a certain kind of arthritis. And among those of my readers who learned with amusement of the Royal trade in 'cramp rings', I wonder how many are wearing a copper ring on their arm to ward off rheumatism? Are we being humbugged once more, or was there, maybe, always something in it?

Let us take another, and extreme, instance from the distant past. It was, and still is, the belief of certain cannibal tribes that eating a brave but fallen foe will endow them with his courage. What could be more absurd? Yet very recent experiments with flat-worms are a little unsettling in this connection. These tiny half-inch creatures are capable of 'learning' certain simple conditioned responses, such as curling up when a light is turned on, instead of reaching towards it which is the creature's normal reaction. When one of these 'trained' flatworms is minced up and given as food to untrained flatworms, the latter 'absorb the learned behaviour along with their food'. Scientific opinion hastens to assure us that this phenomenon occurs only in primitive forms of life and does not apply at the human level. In other words that soldiers cannot absorb the fighting qualities of their enemies by eating them. This seems fairly obvious. But it is perhaps a little less obvious than it was before the flatworm experiments were made.

What then are we to think? Where shall we draw the line? Shall we go back to a sick diet of crushed bugs, urine and old shoes, in the blind hope that these things may somehow do us good? Plainly this is not the answer. We must carry on with our up-to-the-minute double-blind tests and our careful sifting of evidence. It is modern man's unique contribution to knowledge, and in any case this approach has brought us rich and incontrovertible rewards. But we can surely be level-headed about it. The problem of pain and sickness is as old as the human race. We need not assume that until we came along, with our computers and electro-encephalograms, no one had a clue about these things. The insights of other men in other times on the eternal problem of disease are of value precisely because they approached it along a different path from ours. We can discard the unhistorical conviction that the scientific and objective approach to disease is the only one that brings results. We can respect the experts' views without sharing their dogmatism.

5

On Sacred Cows

In the eyes of most scientific authorities to question gravity is a piece of unpardonable levity. The world is with them on this issue, for gravity is not merely a scientific theory, it is a fact of everyday experience. Newton's apple, famous as Adam's, brought home to us all the apparent truth of the matter.

No one has paid much attention to Ruskin's mild comment that Newton had failed to explain how the apple got up there in the first place. Ruskin after all was a writer, not a scientist, and in any case the evidence on the other side is too strong. Look where we will, the paramount power of gravity is revealed. Whatever is erect, whatever springs upward, is seen to be offering a merely temporary defiance of all-conquering gravity. 'What goes up', says Everyman, nodding his head wisely, 'must come down'. Everyman is right. We have to accept that gravity as an unopposed force influencing all bodies to move in a downward direction towards the earth's centre is demonstrably true and irrefutably proved. In fact, ever since Newton's day this theory of gravity (with some later added refinements) has become the lynch-pin holding in place the entire scientific view of the universe.

There is just one awkward circumstance. Apart from a special property recently attributed to a certain type of nuclear energy,* gravity is the only force known to

* One aspect of nuclear force has very recently been advanced as a possible parallel to the 'one-way pull' of gravity. That a

us that is not balanced by an equal and opposite force. In every other field of human observation the world presents itself to us as an intricate balance of opposing tendencies. Theoretically the force opposing gravity should be *levity*. But levity as a force of the same status as gravity has never been accepted by science. More than two hundred years ago it was laid down by the *Accademia del Cimento* of Florence that 'a science firmly based on observation has no right to speak of Levity as something claiming equal right with, and opposite to, Gravity' — and this assertion has never been scientifically refuted or even seriously questioned.

In short, the world-picture we now possess rests upon a startling exception to a general rule. To find that our view of the world is based on an exceptional and unexplained phenomenon seems a little precarious.

When a vital position is seen to be precarious, it is defended with the utmost tenacity. Unopposed gravity is the Sacred Cow of orthodox science, and even to look too closely at it is to ask for your own firing-squad.

Question almost any scientist on the meaning of gravity and he will at once pull a long face, like a country parson asked to explain the doctrine of the Trinity, and murmur something about its being the most mysterious force in the universe. Do not be deceived by his vagueness. Behind it lies an implacable determination to defend the Sacred Cow.

What is the secret of the power that Newton's theory of gravity holds over the minds of men? Earlier chapters of this book offer a possible clue. Apart from its

fraction of such exceptional forces may behave in this way is interesting, but nuclear force has not been on the scientific map long enough for this to be more than a hypothesis which has done nothing yet to weaken the central importance to scientific thought of unopposed gravitational pull.

enormous usefulness in providing an explanation of the physical behaviour of everything from a falling acorn to the orbits of the planets, unopposed gravity is a form of Final Answer. And we have already examined the almost irresistible fascination of this idea, especially for scientists. One of them, you will remember, stated approvingly that all scientific thinkers, including Newton and Einstein, were, 'in a deep sense, Unitarians'. Well, here at last had been discovered a basic, *unitary* fact, proven to the hilt and plain for all the world to see. No wonder that scientists, and the world too, hailed unopposed gravity as a shining truth.

Why should we bother about the possible existence of a force equal and opposite to gravity? Could we not leave all such questions for the experts to quarrel over on their own recondite level? The answer is an unequivocal No. The whole world has accepted Newton's concept of gravity as an unopposed force, and it now enters into every aspect of our thinking and feeling. It has distorted our natural responses to the world we live in, by leading us to believe in a universal force which is *unrhythmical.* For rhythm, coming now to be accepted as an essential factor in all living processes, is born of equal and opposite forces in endless interplay.

The unopposed action of gravity is a pulling-down concept; it *heavies* everything. The notion of 'upwardness' being a living response as primary as gravity no longer enters the human mind. The O.E.D., for instance, says loftily of levity: 'In pre-scientific physics, regarded as a positive property inherent in bodies in different degrees, in virtue of which they tend to rise . . . Obsolete except historically or allusively.' Another magisterial Door-slam. Yet if we look in the right direction, evidence for the existence of levity is as clear and ubiquitous in our everyday experience as the equally valid evidence of gravity.

Take the element of water, which covers nearly three-quarters of the earth's surface. Water runs downhill under the influence of gravity, collecting in the hollows and crevices of the earth in quantities varying from a road-side puddle to the vast basins of the oceans. But water is never completely at rest — not even when locked in wind-forsaken tarns. From its myriad surfaces water streams upward unceasingly as invisible vapour into the upper air, where it is transformed into the incomparable beauty of sailing cloud-scenery; sooner or later to fall back to earth in the form of rain and dew: a continuous circulatory process in which the movement due to levity must necessarily be equal and opposite to the movement due to gravity. Even the apparently dry land takes part in this aqueous rhythm. From every acre of woodland 3,500 gallons of water are sucked into the air on a summer's day. Within the Australian eucalyptus tree the sap, drawn from far under ground by a million rootlets, soars upward for 450 feet, and its water-content then rises invisibly into the upper atmosphere . . . Not water alone, I suggest, but all things in the biosphere are involved in cyclical rhythms, in which the upward movement due to levity is as powerful and as valid as the downward movement due to gravity.

Newton was an outstanding genuis. But like all men he was capable of serious error. As we have seen, he believed in the absolute reality of space and time, a twin conviction which few can now be found to share with him. He also led the world badly astray on the subject of *colours*. He told us, and we all at once believed it, that colours in their totality are contained in light, and by his world-famous experiment 'demonstrated' that a prism *reveals* the colours concealed in light. The fact is, as Professor Ward, Sir Arthur Eddington and others have shown, a prism *manufactures* these colours out of light, which is itself colourless. Goethe pointed this out nearly two hundred years ago, but the world had him ready-labelled as a poet, so no one took any notice.

Is it not possible that Newton was mistaken also about the unopposed nature of gravity? The trouble is that, in this instance, centuries of scientific work depend on his being right. Incidentally, if mistaken he gave his distinguished successor Einstein an unnecessary headache. Einstein is said to have had the greatest difficulty in fitting the unipolar aspect of gravity into his theory of relativity, and to have been unhappy with the result.

Discoveries have often been made on the basis of probability. Gaps in the Table of Atomic Weights led men to look for — and find — undiscovered elements. Astronomical calculations caused observers to search certain empty spaces in the sky where there ought to have been a star — and there was. Would it not be reasonable to look for a counter-balancing force to unipolar gravity on the same principle: that every other known force in the universe is bi-polar? Even if this means bringing a new and disturbing factor into all our calculations?

The refusal to do this results at times in some very curious circumlocutions. In a fine and scholarly book called *Plant and Planet,* Anthony Huxley has nevertheless produced this gem regarding the effect of gravity on plants: 'Thus, the flower-stalk of a peanut starts by being *negatively geotropic,* that is, growing upwards'.

The simple act of growing upward, one of the most natural and primary movements in the world, shared by every living thing, is here described — in deference to the Sacred Cow of gravity — as being 'negatively geotropic'! (As a monument to misdirected thinking this deserves to stand beside Freud's definition of a baby as 'a polymorphous pervert.')

It should be made clear that I have no quarrel with this Sacred Cow as such. She can go on grazing peacefully in her meadow, undisturbed by me, *if only she will allow an Anti-cow of exactly equal status to graze in the same field.* These two animals, though equal in status, are very unlike in appearance. The Sacred Cow of gravity is not really a cow at all, but a rhinoceros, a creature with a single horn on its head and a single idea in its tiny mind: to bear down all opposition by its sheer armoured weight. The Anti-cow, on the other hand, is a springbok, scarce touching the ground with its electric feet, seeming ever on the verge of soaring into illimitable space to which it feels an eternal affinity . . . A curious pair of beasts. But the meadow is vast: it can, it must, contain them both.

I am aware that this is an impertinent chapter. I am calling in question a solid conviction of my far more knowledgeable elders. But after all, it took a cheeky child to tell the world that the Emperor had no clothes on. If we look with a child-like directness at the phenomenal world, does not something in us reject the idea of a universe under the sway of an unopposed force, just as it spontaneously accepts the idea of a universe poised like a ballet-dancer — a delicately living balance of contraries?

No doubt I shall be told that the theory of the unopposed force of gravity is 'no longer a battle-ground'. This is a trump card of spokesmen for the Union of Door-Slammers. 'If you knew what *we* know, they announce, 'you would realise that it is pointless to reopen this subject. It has already been discussed and decided by better-informed brains than yours'. In reply it may be permissible to remind them of what Cromwell said to his stubborn Parliament of Roundheads: 'My brethren, by the bowels of Christ I beseech you, bethink you that you may be mistaken.'

6

In Defence of Play

It is surprising how many otherwise intelligent people are unaware that some things are too serious to be serious about. To unrelieved seriousness the basic existential issues are automatically resistant: they demand an approach which Karl Jaspers has called 'a glancing awareness' of all possible contingencies.

To *decide* to be serious is an excluding attitude of mind. It is a decision to discard in advance a number of alternative approaches to the subject which, in the opinion of the serious thinkers, are irrelevant. People who are in the habit of saying, with a sudden straightening of the features, 'But joking apart —' give themselves away. They convict themselves of seeing life as a grave and earnest affair, lightened here and there by gallant glints of humour, whereas it is nothing of the kind. Life is a shimmering interplay of forces that can at any moment erupt into tragedy, comedy or ecstasy — and only the mercurial spirit of play can cope with these bewildering changes.

That very serious person St. Paul, whose fateful role in shaping world opinion will be considered later, said of himself with unmistakeable satisfaction — 'but when I became a man I put away childish things.' Had he forgotten that 'whosoever shall not receive the kingdom of God as a little child shall in no way enter therein'? It is possible, it is positively easy, to grow up too successfully, to become too competently adult, so that living turns into a goal-seeking, problem-solving, will-driven business in which the quality of magic is missing. The serious-minded thinker, the furrow-browed *Penseur* of Rodin, is obsessed by the search for a Final Answer. He strives unceasingly for this illusory goal, and believes he has no hope of reaching it unless like Ulysses' sailors he stuffs his ears with wax to shut out the Sirens' Song.

*   *   *

There is one apparent exception to this: the jarring event of death. Not by any means your own death, about which it is impossible to be entirely serious without being entirely pompous; but the fading, suffering and death of someone you love, or even of an innocent stranger. To allow the spirit of play to enter into this catastrophe would seem to be less than human. Gravity here enjoys its sting and its undeniable victory. Everything about death and its obsequies proclaims the triumph of gravity in both its meanings. The dead body no longer has any kind of answer to gravity's downward pull; the spade delves down into the ground; the body is lowered into the grave; the earth falls first hollowly, then heavily, on the coffin-lid; and at the finish, despite 'the priest in surplice white, That defunctive music can', the soil is solidly packed down, stamped down, over the inert remains. Here surely is an irrefutable proof of finality, and believers in that kind of Final Answer point to it with a sombre satisfaction.

Indeed, to many such a view seems self-evident. For some men in all ages, and for the majority of the world of today, death is a full stop, a blank wall — the shadow of which darkens all human life and arouses an unassuageable *angst,* however courageously it may be faced. Contemporary man is specifically conditioned to this bleak concept; partly by having been taught to pay no attention to any aspect of Time other than Linear Time (which, of course, Like an Ever-rolling Stream, Bears all its Sons away); partly by his acceptance of the un-opposed action of Gravity, which brings all things low; and finally by the appearance on the scene of that other Sacred Cow which science has recently set up — *Entropy* — the ineluctable, slow heat-death of the universe. Entropy will in time, we are assured on the highest authority, bring to an end not only man but the entire cosmos . . . Seldom can there have been two Cows with less milk to offer mankind. ('Ah', say the distinguished Cow-breeders, 'but supposing it is *true* — would you have us conceal the truth we have discovered because it is depressing?' Saint-Exupéry answers for me. 'Truth', said Exupéry, 'is not what we discover, but what we create.')

Undeniably the death of someone dearly loved weighs on the heart as a crushing victory for the downward drag of Gravity. But to this deduction, without drawing upon religious hopes, there is a valid objection. Gravity has here over-stated its case. Before we can allow ourselves to perform any of these earthy obsequies upon a human being, we have to be absolutely certain that something which was undoubtedly there before is now missing. The legal precautions we take against the possibility of being buried alive are proof of this. Gravity has matters all its own way at death, only because its antagonist has silently slipped away. In their long and perfectly matched chess-game Gravity suddenly finds it can now move the pieces where it will — oblivious of the fact that Levity, its supple adversary, has got up from the table and left the room . . . It is possible, even in the death-chamber, even at the graveside, to force oneself to follow oneself to follow Levity out on its unimaginable journey, and thereby to experience a miraculous lifting of the heart.

*   *   *

Play is a grossly misunderstood activity. The currently accepted definitions for man — Homo Sapiens, Homo Faber, Homo Laborans — are an indication of this. Aristotle's suggestion that man is essentially 'Animal Ridens' is nearer the mark, since no creature but man can laugh. (That is, if we leave out the laugh of the Myna bird — a convincingly human laugh torn completely from its human context — startling and chilling on that very account.) But 'Homo Ludens' has a richer connection with the uniqueness of man. This is the title of a book by Professor Johan Huizinga, which has been hailed as the most important work in the philosophy of history in our century. Whether or not it is that, it is certainly mind-loosening.

The central theme of *Homo Ludens* is the paradox of play as the most serious activity of man, and also, because of play's insistence on rules that must be kept, as the primary shaping force of all civilised behaviour.

Huizinga's book demands to be read in full, not summarised. Here I can only indicate his overall view that play is a vital expression of human freedom; a purely voluntary activity, something we do in our 'free' time. 'Play', he claims, 'is a thing by itself. The play-concept as such is of a higher order than is seriousness. For seriousness seeks to exclude play, whereas play can . . . include seriousness.'

The seriousness of play can be indeed no joke, as in gladiatorial games and mediaeval tourneys, where the stake played for was often nothing less than life itself. The duel, too, despite the solemnity of the participants, is a perfect example of play-activity, with its meticulous rules all designed to ensure 'fair play' — back-to-back position, measured number of paces, and so forth — its umpire and its referees, and even the First Aid box for injured players held in readiness on the side-lines.

The undervalued activity of play, according to this author, has many other qualities of high importance to the human race: 'Play', he says, 'creates order, *is* order . . . The profound affinity between play and order may be the reason why play . . . tends to be beautiful. It may be that this aesthetic factor is identical with the impulse to create orderly form which animates play in all its aspects . . . Play casts a spell over us . . . It is invested with the noblest qualities we are capable of perceiving in things: rhythm and harmony.'

Sophia, the Spirit of Wisdom and mythical consort of God at the time of the Creation, is said to have occupied herself, while God was about the serious business of creating the universe, 'playing before Him at all times; playing in the world': a picturesque way of saying that the spirit of play and the spirit of creation are inseparable.

Let us play.

7

Paradox and Play

No one expects to enjoy a game without first learning the rudiments and understanding the rules. This applies above all to the game of living, which is at once the hardest and simplest of any. While most games have an elaborate set of rules, the game of living, unlike any other that I know of, has but one: to look on it through the eyes of love. This sounds unpardonably sentimental, but it is not. For love, not only of persons but also of things, is equally concerned with the visible and the invisible. It alone is able to maintain this paradoxical point of view, since the eyes of love do not rest on the surface but look simultaneously at, within and through the loved object.

Where this is a human being who loves in return, there can pass between them a continuous flickering interchange of roles and relationships, playing like summer lightning against the dark background of more mundane encounters. In such a union arises uniquely the possibility of permanence without boredom. There are so many delightful variables: parent, adult, child coexist in each partner, masculine and feminine attitudes are found in both. The permutations of these and many other interchanges of role are almost infinite — and only the spirit of play is nimble enough to make the dazzling-swift transitions. The tragedy of most partnerships is that so few of these beguiling variations are recognised and practised. The master-players of love's counterpoint are rare indeed.

As with persons, so with things. We live with our environment as all too often we live with our spouse — without a glimpse of the range and variety of relationships that can be enjoyed. To see the environment so, is to realise the rich responsiveness of the physical world, to be made aware that every object upon which the human eye can rest has a dual quality: it exists not only as a concrete phenomenon but also as a miraculous point of intersection between the temporal and the timeless; the object reveals itself as a symbol, at once concrete and transcendant. The popular notion of symbolism as a profound but rather vague view of life, in which attention is directed away from the actual visible object towards some spiritual truth which it is supposed to illustrate — could hardly be more off the mark. To see everything as a symbol is to intensify almost painfully the vividness and concreteness of the actual. It is to see actuality lit by the radiance of Eternity.

This is true not merely of certain objects but of all that exists. As Karl Jaspers in his penetrating book *Truth and Symbol* has said, 'If we ask about the extent of the realm of symbols, then the answer is: everything can be a symbol.' Archaic man spontaneously saw life in this way, but today perhaps only the artist understands that an object has not merely a concrete actuality, but also a transcendent reality, and perceives that this reality is something which the phenomenal world reveals rather than contains or engenders.

This kind of awareness becomes operative only by means of a certain mode of perception, namely by experiencing the object in a dual sense: with the subliminal as well as the waking part of the mind.

Experiencing with the subliminal part of the mind — what do I mean by this? Something quite definite. To dream is to experience events in this way. But in dream-imagery the experience is *purely* subliminal, as it also is in the disputed field of Extra-Sensory Perception. To experience life with the subliminal part of the mind is, in fact, nothing new. What may be new is the attempt to confront the dual quality in the object with a dual response from the observer; to give a 'binocular' attention — from the subliminal at the same time as the waking levels of the mind — to an object seen as a symbol, that is, seen as an image vividly actual and concrete, yet simultaneously shimmering with the secret life of a different mode of being.

It is now accepted that human beings are bi-sexual in the sense that every man has a feminine and every woman a masculine side. The complementary aspect is submerged; but it exists; and is as real and momentous in its effects as the outward sexual attitude of the individual. I suggest that human consciousness is also bi-sexual, consisting of a waking form which is active and 'masculine', and a subliminal form which is receptive and 'feminine' in quality. In the same way an object, looked upon with love and attention, discloses an actual and concrete aspect which can be described as its 'masculine' component, and an invisible transcendent aspect which exerts the fascinating influence of the 'feminine'.

On this hypothesis, the relationship between man and his environment could be roughly expressed as a parellelogram of forces. To try to represent this subtle interplay by the crude device of a diagram might seem the perfect flower of pedantic folly. Yet I cannot think how else to expose the poverty of the customary responses of man to the world he lives in. It may be worth while to see what comes of such an approach, clumsy as it may be.

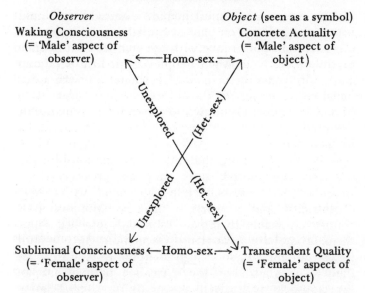

Observer
Waking Consciousness
(= 'Male' aspect of
observer)

Object (seen as a symbol)
Concrete Actuality
(= 'Male' aspect of
object)

←——Homo-sex.——→

Unexplored

(Het.-sex)

Unexplored

(Het.-sex)

Subliminal Consciousness ←—Homo-sex.—→ Transcendent Quality
(= 'Female' aspect of
observer)

(= 'Female' aspect of
object)

From this diagram it will be seen that the ordinary relationship between Observer and Object, is so to speak a 'homosexual' relationship. The active waking side of consciousness, which is its masculine component, normally sees in the object only its concrete actuality, that is, the masculine aspect of the object. Such a relationship, however practical and effective, is by its nature *sterile.*

The second possible relationship, between the subliminal consciousness of the observer (the observer's feminine aspect) and the transcendent quality of the object (which is the object's feminine aspect) is also, it will be noticed, 'homosexual' and therefore in the last resort sterile. In human experience it has, in fact, a ghostly incorporeal quality, since this is the relationship to the world expressed in dreams.

For a fruitful outcome the connection between man

and his environment must include a hetero-sexual link. Either the waking consciousness of the human observer must see and fall in love with the transcendent quality of the object — as when people fall in love with cars and boats and other pieces of machinery; or the subliminal consciousness of the observer must become aware of and be irresistibly drawn to the concrete actuality of the object — as in the case of a Van Gogh painting a kitchen chair.

It is not surprising that these two relationships are relatively unexplored, since they are precisely those which are closely associated in men's minds with at best eccentricity, and at worst — madness. Moreover it is almost impossible to remain calm and detached about them. They have a dangerous fascination which is hard to keep in control, so that prudent minds tend to avoid them altogether. For the masculine part of human consciousness feels itself drawn by an overwhelming curiosity and desire towards the unfathomable feminine mystery of the object; and this is reinforced by the longing of the feminine subliminal consciousness to unite itself to the hard masculine actuality of the object. Man feels the tug, and turns panic-stricken to the one relationship in which he feels safe — the 'man-to-man' relationship between his carefully controlled waking consciousness and the concrete aspects of his environment.

He cannot, of course, entirely ignore the existence either of his own subliminal mind, or of the hidden mystery within the object, but relegates them both to the limbo of dreams and fantasies, with instructions to keep quiet and not interfere with his plans. Only when these plans go seriously wrong is he driven, with much misgiving and every conceivable safe-guard, to call upon the priest or the psychiatrist to help him out of his trouble on a strictly limited and professional basis.

We live too cautiously. I suggest that all these possible reciprocities between man and his environment have in fact an equal validity. As in the point-counter-point of human love, it is a tragedy when they are not all equally honoured and enjoyed. For this to be achieved it is only necessary to quicken every aspect of life with the nimble and mercurial spirit of play.

8

'Dementia Praecox'

Youth is head-over-heels in adolescent love with paradox. Like all head-long passions this has its dangers. And in any case paradox does not care to be wooed in this way. If pursued too eagerly, and merely for its own sake, it leads away from life and into regions of increasing irrelevance.

True paradox appears only after a long blind haul on a logical level: suddenly the mental darkness is split apart, as by a rocket in the night that bursts into a glitter of bright stars. By that brief light a man perceives the reward of his long labour is not, as he had supposed, a finite provable fact, but a dazzling break-through into a new dimension of thought where contraries can co-exist.

Preston Harold — the pen-name of an extraordinary individual who has carried the secret of his identity with him to the grave — makes this point the central theme of his single, formidable book *The Shining Stranger*: 'Truth', he wrote, 'when fully stated must conclude in contradictory truths of equal magnitude, in a bifurcation, a forking outward from the penultimate point of truth, so that the end of it cannot be reached save as a point that opens itself to question.' Carl Jung has said the same thing: 'We have to learn to think in antinomies, constantly bearing in mind that every truth turns into an antinomy if thought out to the end.' The perception and appreciation of true paradox is, in fact, the fine flower of a mature philosophy.

Impatient youth, however, will have none of this.

Having arrived by a leap of intuition (born of the natural affinity of youth for whatever is genuinely new) at an acceptance of the open-ended nature of Reality, it tries naively to embody this discovery here and now, and in the banal terms of everyday life.

In doing so, youth betrays its own insights, and makes rather a fool of itself. Unisex clothes are an unconvincing expression of the paradox involved in the bi-sexual make-up of every human being. Drop-out communes whose activities are for the most part unproductive are not persuasive illustration of the paradoxical truth that the contemplative is of equal survival value to society as the coalminer.

Yet they have a point, these young revolutionaries, though they express it absurdly. Indeed, this absurdity is itself no more than the caricature of a serious fact: that contemporary man is being forced to make a fateful change of direction. He is being dragged, protesting every inch of the way, from the comforting conviction that life is a series of problems waiting for a solution, to the acceptance of life as an endless shimmering balance of contraries.

In panic, men of orthodox mould turn to their old familiar interests and avocations, pursued till so recently with the general approval of society. But now everything they touch seems to change into a grinning caricature of itself, an empty exercise self-consciously carried out under the scornful eyes of youth. There is a crisis of lost confidence in orthodox activities. Politics everywhere are seen to be riddled with corruption, and to offer no more than the choice of equally futile solutions; Big Business loses the mask of benevolence and shows its 'unacceptable face'; war becomes a hideous farce from which every shred of meaning has been finally torn away.

Almost apologetically men continue to carry on these activities, mainly because they don't know what else to do. 'After all', they mutter, 'one must live.' To which youth makes the historic rejoinder, 'I don't see the necessity.' As a retort this is effective, but youth itself has no viable alternative to offer. All it has been able to do so far is to dress up in its rather grubby motley and dance, clumsily enough, on the grave of the old certainties.

The old certainties are dead all right. They are dead because they were sustained by an idea that has become discredited. Preston Harold has called this idea the Messianic Delusion. The victim of the Messianic Delusion holds the unshakeable conviction that to all ultimate questions of the meaning of existence there is in the last resort a true and final answer, and that somewhere there must be found, or has been found, a Leader who possesses it. In vain almost all the Founders of the great religions have taught otherwise. Laotse and Buddha each in their turn strove to undermine this fatal expectation. The Founder of Christianity, though having Messiahship practically thrust upon him by the long-cherished hopes of his contemporaries, spent and finally gave his life in repudiation of the title. And now, partly through the mind-liberating concepts of current physics, their message appears at last to have a chance of being understood and accepted.

It is to the credit of contemporary youth to have caught a glimpse of the world-mutating nature of the idea that life is an open-ended process — however crass their interpretation of it may be. But their cardinal error has been to jump to the conclusion that because the old certainties are dead, there is no point in continuing the old activities. This is a childish conclusion. The situation is more subtle. To support the number of people now on earth, the traditional activities must not only be continued, but extended, if universal, senseless suffering is to be avoided. Despite the drop-out protest, economic trends will go on much as before, look much as before. But there is now a possibility of a crucial difference. The actors on the human stage, both young and old, *may grow up*. They may find themselves with a totally altered feeling about the play, and about their own and the other actors' parts in it. It may be seen at last that the play is *not* the thing. What matters is the players' attitude to the play.

A tale was once told of a poor country curate who was bored and exasperated by his petty parochial duties, though he carefully concealed this and was highly regarded by everyone as a holy young man. Through his mind secretly but ceaselessly ran Satanic images of the life he would lead if he were rich; of the shocks he would delight to give everyone by his wild and profligate life . . . the cars and yachts and country-houses he would own . . . the wits and gamblers and demi-mondaines who would throng his salons . . . One day a merchant-millionaire in Shanghai, who had always silently admired the self-denying life of his parson-cousin, died and left the curate his entire fortune . . . *Now,* thought the curate, *I'll show them* . . . After sleepless nights considering all the publicly scandalous exploits he could now indulge in, he suddenly realised that the wickedest, and therefore most satisfactory thing he could do would be to tell no one of his legacy and − carry on being a holy young curate.

This rather evil little story serves merely to illustrate the point that it is possible to do precisely what one was doing before, but with an entirely altered feeling towards it; and that this can be both more rewarding and more satisfying than behaving in a flamboyantly different style. The wall-eyed bourgeois and the pie-eyed hippy are not the sole alternatives open to the human race. There is another and interior dimension of living.

The vision of Everyman going to work, like the curate, with his tongue in his cheek, may seem pure phantasy. Are blast-furnace workers going to sweat their lives away, commuters to squeeze themselves night and morning into smelly, suffocating railway carriages, unless they believe in the necessity of what they are doing? But again, it is not as simple as this. What is here suggested is that men might adopt the attitude of an actor to his work. To be acceptable as an actor is of considerable importance, both to himself and his dependants. And to be an acceptable actor he must take in all seriousness his own part, his relationship with the other actors, and the play itself. But if he begins to confuse his part in the play with his actual life, as Noel Coward reminded us in *Spring Fever,* he becomes at once irrelevant and absurd.

This paradox of the actor playing his part for all it is worth, but never forgetting that behind him is only a painted back-drop, is a paradigm of the way man might live. To live so requires only that a man shall be always a size larger than his job.

But man — especially middle-aged man — just doesn't live that way. In essence this is what youth is so contemptuous about: that we take our fancy costumes and painted scenery for real. Youth is out to ridicule our fancy costumes by caricaturing them, and to demonstrate the flimsy nature of the scenery by smashing it up; hence the apparently insane phenomena of seat-slashing, window-breaking, train-wrecking, and beating up of harmless passers-by. Naturally such goings-on attract the enthusiastic cooperation of nit-wit rowdies, petty criminals and the mentally unbalanced, and this confuses the issue for many. But the occasional glimpse of unconscious meaning behind all these ugly activities should not be missed.

It is a meaning that has close connections with the meaning of a mass outbreak from gaol. What moves convicts to the forlorn attempt to escape *en masse* is not poor conditions or bad food, though these are often cited as causes, but a deep inchoate conviction that it is a monstrous thing, *whatever reasons may be given,* for one group of human beings to be seized and locked up by another group of human beings. The social rights and wrongs of the matter do not at such a moment concern them. They are obsessed by the fact of loss of freedom, and are easily convinced that the Authorities who have done this to them, and have conned the world into believing that this is the right way to deal with certain situations, should be resisted with unlimited violence. It may be wrong-headed, but it is understandable.

Contemporary youth has a comparable feeling of claustrophobia, and has as little idea as the escaping convict what to do with his freedom. But the depth and completeness of his rejection of the accepted social order should be recognised. Compared with it, such an anti-social exploit as the Great Train Robbery creates an almost cosy feeling. We know very well what the Train Robbers were after. Like the majority of us they were after *money* — only they wanted it quick and without working for it. Their elaborate plans and split-second timing were an admission of the power and permanence of Civil Authority and the Social Order. 'Cops and Robbers' is a game we can all understand and even, from the security of our own fireside, enjoy.

But the phenomenon of the 'bovver-boys' of Great Britain — matched in America by the Hell's Angels, and in Russia by the *stilyagi* or 'style-boys' — presents us with something far more disquieting: violence for its own sake, or even more chillingly, 'for a giggle', senseless destruction, crime without wish for reward, a contemptuous flouting of even the basic rules of human behaviour. We have an uneasy feeling that they have crossed an invisible frontier into a region where we can no longer communicate with them, where our praise is a sour joke and our punishments are irrelevant. They have dropped out of our world.

The general dismay aroused by this situation is a little surprising. There is nothing new in the drop-out phenomenon, except its size. We have had tramps around for centuries.

In the Seventeenth Century the word *tramp* described an "acceptable" kind of person, one who 'roamed the country', as the O.E.D. puts it, 'especially in search of work.' This socially reassuring intention masked for a time from the Authorities the deplorable fact that such people had no settled home; but the truce between tramps and society was brief. Even by 1630 tramps were being classed, with vagrants and vagabonds, as 'rascally, worthless individuals leading a disreputable life.' Trade organisations later tried to save the status of those who were artisans genuinely looking for work by issuing *Tramping-Cards* entitling the holder to public maintenance. It was in vain. Tramps became, and have remained to this day, outcasts from society, subject to the varying penalties prescribed by local magistrates. The public conscience has never felt quite at ease with this summary classification. Few citizens can walk past the bleared, alien, stone-eyed face, so close for a moment to their own, without either giving money or hastily rationalising to themselves why they do not. The reason for this unease lies in what could be called the Tramp's Paradox.

In Genet's rather repulsive book *The Thief's Journal* this paradox is suddenly revealed in one simple phrase, which illuminates from a new angle the strange, abject self-martyrdom of tramps anywhere in the world. Genet is commenting on his sense of discomfort during a brief spell of comparative prosperity. *'I lacked'*, he says, *'a taste for earthly happiness.'*

This is the meaningful epitaph of the tramp. It carries us to the core of the enigma of self-chosen degradation. It is precisely this which makes them incomprehensible and a little frightening to the rest of us. Because we know that in a way they are right in turning aside from our unresting pursuit of goods and status. Their distaste for these things is shared by the saints. In this one sense they are stronger than us, and shame us. But it is always possible to shrug off and forget these merely occasional encounters. What is dismaying about the contemporary drop-out phenomenon is that there are so many of them.

Not that tramps and hippies are synonymous terms. There is a crucial difference. The heart of the true tramp is emptied of both hope and despair. He has passed, while still alive, to the Farther Shore, which gives his miserable state a formidable quality. The despair of the young drop-out is largely histrionic, and covers an innocent hope, natural to youth, that his revolt will lead to a better world. But tramps and hippies have one thing in common — a deep rejection, cost what it may, of the values of contemporary society.

These comments on drop-out behaviour are intended only to open up lines of discussion on this complex phenomenon. Other possibilities exist. There is a form of mental disorder, for example, which involves a similar rejection of accepted social values. Indeed, the heading of this chapter carries the suggestion that these drop-out groups may be suffering from a kind of mass schizophrenia. It could be so. Their behaviour does conform to the classic distinction between psychosis and neurosis —

71

that the psychotic has become what is called 'inaccessible'; that is, has passed into a region where we can no longer communicate with him. But we should also take note of the fact that an influential school of contemporary thought headed by R.D. Laing believes that schizophrenia of early onset is not an illness at all, but a profound reaction to the unconscious attitudes and pressures of their elders. The ball may be in the older generations' court, after all.

9

Youth, War and Myth

Supposing Dr. Laing is right, and the elderly at heart are responsible for the intransigence of youth — as youth itself is never tired of telling them. The seniors who can accept this are apt to look at each other with shocked and anxious faces, asking *"But what have we done?"* After all, they meant well, and tried hard; secretly they have a mildly heroic image of themselves, having battled through two major wars and won them both. Congratulatory post-war slogans still ring, though faintly, in their ears — 'We Did our Bit, We Never Closed, We Went Without to Win the War' — and now they try with a rather pathetic dignity to conceal their dismay that their children, even of the non-delinquent kind, are not in the least impressed.

Well, what *have* they done? Could it be that in spite of all the blood and sweat and tears they shed, they failed utterly, not merely once but twice, to grasp the meaning of the disaster that had befallen them? — And that then, spiritually and physically exhausted by the two greatest conflicts in human history, they allowed at the close of fighting something infinitely precious — born bloodily, as in physical birth, from the travail of the nations — to disappear yet again from their way of life? And that precisely this is what has set the teeth of the children on edge? If so, then what is it that youth's bizarre behaviour is trying to bring back?

I suggest it is the mythic element in human life.

Such a suggestion will at once raise many eyebrows.

73

The word *myth* is now a mere synonym for 'a fiction'. It's only a myth, people say, meaning that there is no truth in it. A distinguished American Professor of Literature actually described a passage in Coleridge as a 'howling myth', thus putting myth on a par with a schoolboy 'howler'. Even the Shorter O.E.D. is content to define it as '1. a purely fictitious event. . . 2. a fictitious or imaginary person or object.'

It is well to remember that there have been other views. Aristotle, that master of the objective approach to life, who gave Western culture a bias in favour of the strictly factual from which it is only now beginning to recover, rather surprisingly declared 'the lover of myths, which are a compact of wonders, is by the same token a lover of wisdom.' The world-famous myths recorded by Plato plainly carried in his mind a more than 'purely fictitious' value. Leaping the centuries, old Noah Webster, in some ways a far more perceptive lexicographer than the painstaking editors of the O.E.D., came a little nearer the mark in defining myth as 'a story, the origin of which is forgotten . . . associated with religious rites and beliefs.'

Among contemporary writers Carl Jung bluntly declares — 'Myth is not fiction: it consists of facts that are continually repeated, and can be observed over and over again. It is something that happens to man, and ordinary men have mythical fates just as much as the Greek heroes do.' And again, at the very end of his life — 'Myth is the revelation of divine life in man. It is not we who invent myth, rather myth speaks to us.' Ananda Coomoraswamy is equally unequivocal: 'Myth embodies the nearest approach to absolute truth that can be stated in words.'

Such lone witnesses could be multiplied, but perhaps the present position is best summed up in the deceptively mild observation of Professor Morton Kelsey, a contemporary theologian — 'The understanding of myth as a religious language, expressing the spiritual reality within and from beyond man, is not very much known today.'

Welcome as they are, these statements are themselves incomplete. Myth is not solely 'a revelation of the divine life in man.' It is also a revelation of the demonic life that is in him. The timeless function of myth is to bring home to men the unbelievable range of behaviour of which ordinary human nature is capable, and to remind them that only in the fierce fires of these extremes of experience can the divinity of man be forged.

Most human beings don't want to know about this. They want to live and love and die among the cautious middle octaves of experience. In Rilke's phrase, 'They smudge away the feelings that surprise. And all their words are safe as an old tune.' The message of myth is that life on this level is totally meaningless. Contemporary youth is shouting, rather hysterically, the same thing.

The fact is, man cannot live without myths. But repeatedly he tries to. History records a periodic appearance and disappearance of the mythic element in human life.

Tragedy can so arise, for when this vital element has been repressed it is apt to break out in catastrophic forms. The two most determined attempts to live without the sustaining power of myth have followed the two greatest wars in history. This was predictable. Global war acts like a depth-charge in the deep waters of the unconscious, bringing up to the surface of life huge, inchoate forces for both good and evil that would otherwise have never seen the light of day. This is a terrifying and bewildering experience. To the eyes of reason global war is a night-mare acted out in full consciousness, a gross and lunatic insult to the rational conduct of life. War is both of these things — but it is something else. It is the stern revenge of long-imprisoned energies in the human mind. War forces man into the mythic style of life in its most savage and destructive form.

In this lurid atmosphere certain tough spirits find their metier, either for good or ill, and thrive amazingly; but the rest of mankind are sickened and exhausted. And when at last the peace that is no peace settles like a raw-necked vulture on the mortuary scene, men turn massively away from what they conceive to be the demonic world of myth. With weary bodies and tired minds they struggle to establish a way of life in which it has no part. In short, war gives myth a bad name.

The middle generation of today either escaped this experience altogether or recalls it confusedly as an exciting time when you might be hauled out of bed in the middle of the night, wrapped in a prickly blanket and bundled into a candle-lit cellar, to hear as in a dream a high, thin, ululating wail — wrung from the tortured spirit of the night — followed by enormous bangs and crumps and the earth-rocking rumble of collapsing buildings; all this mysterious commotion being sweetly offset by the miracle of being out of bed at all at such an hour, and of being inexplicably rewarded for it with biscuits and hot cocoa. A blurred memory of such nights and days, belonging to the world of myth rather than everyday life, may well underlie, in that particular generation, their typically cynical view of post-war aspirations.

To others, born long after the debilitating conflict, the attitude of their elders is simply unbelievable. Never having experienced it, they make no allowance for exhaustion and disillusionment. They passionately reject all middle-of-the-road philosophies. For them the Golden

Mean is born of the collision of extremes; as practised by their elders it seems to them far from golden and depressingly mean. All around them, especially in the field of science, they see long-locked doors being triumphantly burst open, and they themselves have only to see a locked door to feel a claustrophobic urge to smash their way through it — even though what lies beyond may be disintegration or death. And owing to their ignorance and impatience this is just what too often awaits them. Yet what is intended by their rash experiments to reach a new kind of awareness is by no means always ignoble. At their best they are saying that if man is to survive he must raise his sights beyond purely practical considerations and begin to live in more accord with the unexplored heights and depths of his nature. This is also the meaning of myth.

For the world of myth is a world of mingled beauty and terror, where the impossible happens as a matter of course, where rational expectations are either crushed or extravagantly rewarded without apparent reference to human notions of justice, where man-sized standards and values seem no longer to apply. It exists to remind us that the ordered universe that human reason yearns for, where man develops gradually towards perfection, human truth and justice are in permanent session, and history 'broadens down from precedent to precedent' — is a fantasy that can never be more than locally and fleetingly realised. Myth tells us that if life is to have meaning it must rest on something altogether different — more beautiful, more terrifying, more inscrutable — than this cosy but all-too-human vision. In a word, the world of myth is a world of paradox, and as such is mortally humiliating to humanist pretensions.

Perhaps the supreme expression in literature of the encounter between the rational human mind and the world of myth is contained in the Book of Job, where Job's undeniably reasonable reproaches to his God are swept aside by a Voice that answers him out of a whirl-wind. Coming with magical 'rightness' from the heart of a whirlwind, the Voice does not deign to meet Job's arguments with counter-arguments. It simply empties them of meaning by opening a door on a world of al-together different dimension; on a landscape where human reason stands suddenly dwarfed and dismayed before the grandeur of happenings that are completely outside its grasp: the huge thrust and counter-thrust of the forces that underpin the fragile stage where reason struts and plans . . . 'Tell me', says the Voice, 'whereon are the foundations of the earth fastened, or who laid the cornerstone thereof? Where is the way where light dwelleth, and as for darkness, where is the place thereof? Canst thou bind the sweet influences of the Pleiades or loose the bands of Orion? Have the gates of death been opened to thee?' It is a crushing indictment of man's cosmic impotence, and reason can do no more than accept it in silent despair.

But to paradox nothing is a final truth — not even the Voice out of a whirlwind. Opposed eternally to this Voice are the illimitable possibilities of man, and his triumphant shout — 'Whatever flames upon the night, man's own resinous heart has fed!'

These two great antagonistic claims roll like thunder through the universe, and together form the ultimate paradox of the human condition. It has been perfectly expressed in a phrase from the Kabbala: 'Man holds in his right hand a morsel of dust, and in his left a cluster of stars.'

10

Nature's Monstrous Failures

We would do well to keep in mind the Kabbalistic paradox; for looked at purely biologically the human race is in a sorry mess. If we are nothing more than a product of the evolutionary process, the evidence suggests that Nature's experiment with the human species is heading for failure, and she may well be tempted to give some different species a chance.

Life experiments endlessly — and ruthlessly. The workshop of nature is strewn with discarded models. By looking back, her latest experiment, Man, can observe this process clearly enough. Yet he behaves as if what is now going on around him — in particular the emergence of human conurbations of ever expanding size and inner complexity — were entirely his own idea and under his own control. This could be a tragic misapprehension.

It is also an error of fact. Life has tried her hand many times before, as with bees, ants, termites, in the production of communities which are far more closely knit, far more fully integrated than any human group. So much so that these insect communities appear to some scientists rather as one purposive indidivudal than as a swarm of separate insects. 'Perhaps the only solution', suggests Maeterlinck in *The Life of the White Ant*, 'is to consider the hive, the ant-hill and the termitary as a single individual with its parts scattered abroad; a single living creature that has not yet become, or has ceased to be, combined or consolidated.'

History is said to repeat itself. So does prehistory.

Life is trying the same trick with man now as she tried with insects about a hundred million years ago. In the not inconsiderable interval she has, of course, tested out other ideas. Starting, for example, from microscopic unicellular organisms she experimented for geological periods of time in the direction of larger and more complex individuals. This went well for a while and, encouraged by success, Life began eventually to create veritable giants, dinosaurs, brontosaurs, tyrannosaurs and their like, prodigious creatures of a pre-human era whose nightmare skeletons still threaten us — from the glass cases of museums. Their failure was not simply a matter of size alone, but of size in relation to structure. The price of survival for all living creatures is the maintenance of a right proportion between size and structure. This applies to animalcule as well as to dinasaurs. The breathing apparatus of insects, for instance, is unsuited to any but miniature forms of life. A man-sized wasp or spider is luckily a biological impossibility, at least on this earth. In the case of such creatures as these, however, Life has sensibly come to terms with their limitations, and thereby maintained them at a safe though humble level. But in the enormous armoured land-animals of prehistory Life's experiments overshot the mark. The tiny brains of those great reptiles were inadequate to the nutritional problems presented by their size, and in the struggle for existence they were finally defeated. Strangely enough — perhaps to remind us of what she can do when she has a mind to it — Life has preserved in equatorial waters just one creature, the sperm-whale, which is by far the greatest of all mammals that have ever existed, heavier by many times than any pre-historic beast. But even this impressive survivor is now at last on the point of extinction.

Learning from these monstrous failures Life seems to

have dropped the whole idea of breeding giant individuals, and turned back to the creation of groups, particularly human groups. Under her invisible orchestration human families began to combine for mutual protection and advancement; tribes and nations appeared on earth, and later towns and cities. Through immense periods of time this proved a most successful experiment; especially in the creation of cities, which gradually developed into powerful, pulsing, pullulating organisms, each with its unique and recognisable 'personality'. In a new form the giant organism had returned to earth, and reigned in triumph over all living things. To be the free-born citizen of a great city became the proudest boast of a man — even of a St. Paul, who turned on his accusers once with the arrogant cry, 'I am Paul of Tarsus, a citizen of no mean city.'

Through the slow centuries the cities grew, these huge sessile creatures, in strength and valour, in beauty and balanced complexity . . . Babylon, Alexandria, Athens, Rome: Pekin, Moscow, Venice, San Francisco . . . O, in their heyday, cities! — sleek magnificent animals sprawling indolently across famous rivers, poised with the pride of antlered stags on mountain-tops, stretched out like great basking cats along the incandescent edges of the sea . . . Until at last in our unlucky day they begin to get unwieldy, to grow congested and plethoric, afflicted by those identical troubles that beset and ultimately eliminated the giant reptiles of prehistory.

In all essentials the archaic tragedy repeats itself. Filled with fear and despair the city-monsters of today are turning upon each other. The crash of hard colliding bodies, the ear-splitting din of hunger-maddened dinosaurs battling in the Mesozoic swamp, the outlandish cries of the dying; all this is heard again in the crash of masonry and the white flash and following roar of the great engines of destruction which the city-monsters hurl against each other; while high above the battle-ground sounds a wailing of air-raid sirens — the hopeless, ululating cry wrung from the heart of a stricken monster.

But the battles of the city-monsters are as meaning-less as were those of the dinosaurs, for victor and van-quished are equally doomed unless by some miracle they can restore the vital proportion between size and structure. The dinosaurs failed in this; can the city-monsters succeed? Here lies the crux.

As the myth of Babel fore-tells, there is a point be-yond which human powers of organisation become increasingly inadequate to meet the problems of further growth. The difficulties become *more than man-sized.* The largest human colonies are now confronted with just such a situation. Consider in this light the living body of a modern city. The myriads hurrying to and fro within its congested bulk are the carriers of oxygen to its limbs and vital organs. Venous and arterial channels bear these corpuscles about their business by a steady circadian pulsation, a diastole-systole of the city's heart; drawing in the jostling crowds each morning, thrusting them out each night, in a complex circulatory motion which can function smoothly only if perfectly balanced.

Here the inexorable law of size in relation to structure comes once more into play. For already the point has been reached at which the conduits are manifestly in-capable of carrying their corpuscular traffic — and there is no more space within the animal's body for their further enlargement or multiplication. The tiny collec-tive brain of the great beast has not the wit to solve the problem. Short of ideas, and of breath, the sick city-monster lies panting and half paralysed, at one moment glaring round in impotent fury, at another feeding mind-lessly through force of habit on whatever still lies within its reach — thus fatally accelerating the course of its grave disorder.

The outlook is unpromising. For Life, so versatile in new expedients to save her favoured creations, is showing signs of growing tired of this particular experiment. Here and there she is beginning to revert to smaller, simpler groupings. Where fragmentation of larger communities is possible, as in the colonial empires, it is already occurring. It is true that Life has made one or two efforts in an opposite direction; that is, to create superior centres of intelligence, capable of dealing with the problems that lie obviously outside the range of the individual city-monster. The abortive League of Nations was one such centre, the current phenomenon of UNO is another. But her heart hardly seems to be in it. And in any case the greed and pride and lust for autonomy of the great communities give little promise of success in this direction. It would be simpler, Life may have already concluded, to put into the myopic brains of these clumsy creatures the means of their own swift mutual annihilation; and start afresh.

As ever, Life is prodigal of means to her own private ends. Not content with the multi-megaton bomb, she is now encouraging the emergence of yet more sinister modes of mutual destruction. In secret laboratories throughout the world men are at this moment developing a range of chemical and bacillary weapons whose lethality appals even their own insensate creators. Once decided on the liquidation of an unpromising project, Life makes a good job of death.

But supposing that even at this late hour Life changes her mind, and resolves to continue the human group experiment. Given time she would undoubted succeed. Gradually there would evolve, as in the nightmare vision of Pere Teilhard du Chardin, a super-intelligence, not set up in some international centre, nor lodged in any single mind, but permeating the community: an all-powerful, prescient, implacable group-mind, whose decisions can only be accepted unquestioningly by the individual. Necessarily so, since by that time individuals will have relegated to it, centuries before, the functions of thought and will. Such a super-intelligence will be permanently unchallengeable, for it will rule from inside as well as outside each individual. It will be everywhere — and nowhere. There is after all nothing new in this. The collective intelligence which controls the hive or the termitary has this mysterious invisible and unquestionable power.

These things have not happened to us yet. There is still time to decide — *is this what we want*? But they may not be far off. One contemporary writer has seen humanity caught already in the grip of an unseen yet pervasive power with which it is impossible to contend; and it drove him to despair and death. Kafka's tremendous, suffocating books communicate perfectly the panic horror of the moment when man begins to guess that the very essence of himself, the power to will, to decide, to feel, even to realise the loss of these faculties, is slipping out of his grasp and sliding smoothly into invisible waiting hands whose purposes, perhaps hostile, at best indifferent, must be for ever unknown to him.

*　　*　　*

Three possibilities, then, are open to modern man. We can continue as we have started — bombing, poisoning and infecting each other till death do us part, leaving Life a free hand either to begin again with the remnants of the human race, or to experiment with some altogether different species. Many already believe this to be the destiny of our world — and try not to think about it. Or we can recognise the fatal imbalance between size and structure in our present communities, and choose consciously to disintegrate into smaller and more manageable groups. But this is manifestly a pipe-dream. As the world knows, the world's population can now be supported only by the interlocked resources of huge industrial groups — business-monsters that are the unwieldy progeny of the city-monsters. Even if we would, we cannot go back.

There remains apparently only the third possibility: a sacrifice of individual values, and a passive human co-operation in Life's current tentative moves towards a super-intelligent group-mind, of which the individual is merely the acquiescent instrument. This is the goal towards which the contemporary planner unconsciously strives; perhaps in the long run the most hideous solution of all.

Three very disagreeable answers to the problem. Yet there are a number of intelligent people, some eminent philosophers among them, who are perfectly content with this conclusion. It fits their bleak negativism. 'There you are', these wan fellows say, 'that proves it. We always knew it was as bad as that,' and they break into a loud dry cackle that sounds very unlike human laughter, but very like the noise of a couple of skeletons copulating on a corrugated iron roof.

Undreamed of by them, there is another way of looking at these things. When a solution appears to lead to nihilism it is a safe assumption that the lines of approach are inadequate. Some factor of primary importance has not been taken into account. It is as if a two-dimensional mind were facing a three-dimensional crisis. This is the predicament of contemporary man.

Could it be that the daunting difficulties now crowding in upon the bewildered human race are designed to awaken man to this fact? Is it possible that they carry a numinous command that man must now reach a new relationship to the world around him, and that to do this he must accept the paradox of dealing with his external problems by giving priority, not to them, but to the *mind* that is trying to grapple with them? For hardly a beginning has yet been made to bring the illimitable inner world that has recently been opened to us, the world of the unconscious, the world of dreams, into living contact with everyday life. Within the mind of Everyman there are untried forms of apprehension, altogether different from waking consciousness, and free of the waking mind's anxious pre-occupation with space and time. They are indeed so different that he is rightly afraid of them. Yet it could be that this is the moment when man must take the desperate risk of permitting a break-through of the imagery of the dreaming mind into everyday life — the risk of allowing the dark sun of the unconscious to rise above the mind's horizon and irradiate the world we live in with 'a new and terrible beauty'. Undeniably this is a dangerous remedy (although there are contemporary painters who show us that it can be done); but the disease is equally dangerous. And it is possible that only an awareness thus widened and enriched can find answers to problems that are so manifestly growing beyond the grasp of purely practical minds.

A Fresh Look at the Dreaming Mind

We cannot but respect the grave-faced searching for the Aristotelian *causa efficiens,* the patient unravelling of the tangled skein of life, which is the hall-mark of the scientific research-worker. Without these dedicated men the triumphs of modern technology, such as they are, could never have come to pass. We have to admire their tireless pursuit of logical solutions — just as we have to applaud the unflagging efforts of a bumble-bee to escape through a window which, did it but know, is open at the top.

This unflattering comparison is not an attempt to de-value the logical approach, but to *relativise* it, to make room in the human mind for its complement. I suggest that the extra-sensory experience of dreaming is this complementary factor. It is the escape-route, the window-chink, for the bewildered logical faculty, as it buzzes angrily against the invisible pane of glass which separates it for ever from the living world . . . A few great scientists have always known this to be true. Kékulé, the famous Professor of Chemistry in Ghent University, once ended his address to a gathering of distinguished scientists with the words, '*Let us learn to dream, gentlemen.*'

It is unlikely that Kékulé intended to discredit the logical approach. He was simply reminding his eminent colleagues that the discoveries reached by the logical approach alone are necessarily on the same level as the premises from which they start. A breakthrough can occur only when the train of logical thought unexpectedly collides with an idea coming from a totally different direction. Since the conscious mind operates exclusively on the causal principle, such an idea must come from a region of the mind not normally employed in conscious thought: that is to say, from the unconscious.

Dreams are the insights of the unconscious made visible. They should be treated with respect, handled with gentleness, for they are envoys from a land still as remote from us and as fabulous as the realm of Prester John. Paradoxically this far country is also literally within us, 'nearer', as a 13th century Persian poet has said, 'than the neck-artery.' To question messengers from so mysterious a source on a purely rational level for purely practical ends, without at least attempting to discover what light they might throw on the pseudo-certainties of the waking mind, is surely the height of unwisdom. Dreams should be studied, not merely for their immediate utility-value but also for evidence of the mode of operation of the dreaming mind and its special use of images and language. In regard to dream-language we have behaved too long like day-trippers to the Continent, willing to learn only such phrases as will enable us to buy some trifle at a cheap rate of exchange and smuggle it home through Customs.

It is not easy to give the dreaming mind this disinterested attention, for dreams have the spell-binding power of all true symbols. It is also risky, since dream-language is a standing insult to the process of logical thinking, which is perhaps the proudest and most passionately guarded achievement of the human race. Indeed only a fool could deny the value of thinking conducted under the rules of logic, or wish to overthrow them. The fear that this might happen is the origin of the bitter opposition and scorching contempt with which many cultivated minds regard those who dare to look elsewhere even for a moment. Nevertheless, to do so is the specific necessity of our time.

It may seem perverse to suggest that the most important aspect of the dreaming mind is suffering from neglect — at a time when contemporary psychiatry is so busily concerned with the meaning of dreams; and equally perverse to say that in the past also this aspect has been consistently ignored — in face of the perennial fascination that dreams have had for man since his first stumbling appearance on earth. But the fact is, both past and present uses of dreams have been either exclusively practical or strictly therapeutic. The dream has never yet been explored as an experience in itself, as a glimpse of a world 'altogether other', as a providential means of surpassing the limits of ordinary consciousness. Experiments in this direction have been made with the help of hallucinogenic drugs, but dreams are not to be confused with hallucinations. A drug 'trip' is a fascinating, but not exclusively human experience. It is now known that about twenty species of animals are in the habit of taking hallucinogenic drugs. Elephants, for example, are addicted to the fruit of the Umgana tree, after which they can be observed 'staggering about, playing huge antics, and screaming so as to be heard miles off . . .' Plainly they are enjoying themselves no end, but it is doubtful if they are searching for the meaning of life.

The therapeutic use of dreams, from the snake-pit techniques of Aesculapius to the contemporary analyst's couch, is common knowledge. But it may be less well-known that from the practical stand-point also dreams have always been of immense importance to men from the most primitive times. In the central deserts of Africa and the jungle uplands of Malaya pockets of Stone Age survivors are still to be found who look on dreams as their chief guide to daily living. The anthropologist Patrick Noone stayed with one Malayan group called the Temiars who made no decisions of any kind, personal or communal, without the guidance of a dream. But such a statement gives no indication of the astonishing subtlety and skill with which the Temiars related their conscious lives to the world of dreams. It is possibly true to say that their *practical* rapport with the forces of the dreaming mind has never been equalled. To the Temiars dream-images are representations of spirit-forces of enormous power — ambivalent forces capable of either great evil or great good. To draw out their beneficent side it is necessary, they say, to face and master them. This view manifestly enhances both the reality of dreams and the reality of the dangers to be encountered in the world in which we live. The Temiar sees the dangerous aspects of the world, mirrored in dreams, as *challenges to his courage.* These dangerous forces are willing, perhaps even eager, to become his powerful allies, but only if he is capable of proving that he is their master: surely a vigorous and constructive approach both to dreams and to life.

Contemporary psychiatry's concept of a mature human being is of a man who understands the world as an arena made insecure chiefly by the fears and complexes in his own mind. Its aim, particularly in psychoanalysis, is to expose the baseless or childish nature of these fears by analytic treatment. Or in the case of the non-analytical, drug-orientated psychiatrist, to seek the biochemical flaws in the patient's metabolism which have created the emotional disturbance, and to treat these flaws by appropriate drugs.

The Temiar's idea of a mature human being is of a

man who lives in an actually dangerous world and by facing these truly dangerous forces with courage persuades them to become his allies. And he develops this kind of courage by his responses to these forces as they appear in dreams. *He uses dreams as a practice-ground for life.* He has been shown how to do this from childhood. As Richard Noone writes, quoting from his brother's notes: 'The Temiar child is taught to struggle against dream-images until he is convinced, and his parents and advisers are agreed, that a particular image has become genuinely benign, and is acting in his interests.' The Temiars have in fact anticipated Kékulé's advice by encouraging their children to 'learn to dream'. (Incidentally, Noone was so captivated by the gaiety, sanity and purity of their dream-based life-style, that he forsook his Cambridge University background, threw in his lot with the Temiars, and married the chieftain's daughter.)

At a supposedly more sophisticated level, the influence of dreams on the practical conduct of life pervades the sacred literature of many cultures. Joseph's interpretation of Pharaoh's famous cattle dream, for example, had the remarkably practical effect of forecasting and thereby avoiding the consequences of a potentially disastrous Egyptian drought. In the New Testament dream-warnings are recorded no less than five times in the first two pages. And they were crucial warnings. If each one had not been listened to, and acted upon, the whole course of Western religious history for the following two thousand years could have been basically altered. As knowledge of the Bible can no longer be assumed, they are worth summarising.

1. Joseph was warned in a dream that the pregnancy of his wife-to-be, Mary, was by the Holy Ghost. If he had not listened to and acted upon this dream, Mary,

according to the moral principles of the time, would have been 'put away privily'.

2. Herod's envoys whom he sent to find the new-born Jesus so that he could destroy Him, were warned in a dream not to tell Herod. They obeyed this dream.

3. Joseph was told in a dream to flee with his wife and child into Egypt — and immediately took the dream's advice.

4. When in Egypt, another dream informed Joseph that it was now safe to come back to Israel. He began the return.

5. During his return journey he was warned in yet another dream that Herod's son would be equally hostile, and that to save their lives he must turn aside to Nazareth and live there. He did so.

Whether these stories are fact or fable is of little importance in this context. Either way they attest the value given to the dreaming mind in those days as a guide to the immediate problems of life. A fascinating book called *Dreams: The Dark Speech of the Spirit,* by Morton Kelsey, Director of Education at Notre Dame University, Indiana, draws attention to the overwhelming influence of dreams and visions on the Jewish and Christian communities from Genesis to Aquinas. Professor Kelsey incidentally exposes the quiet smothering of this influence by theologians of the present day. Many leading members of the Door-Slammers' Union wear a clerical collar.

*   *   *

Dreams, then, can guide, can heal, can warn. They have been so used for centuries, and contemporary interest in these functions is very much alive. But what concerns us in this chapter is something entirely different: *the dream as evidence.*

To speak of evidence suggests the law-courts. In a court of law such a statement would be quickly pounced upon by opposing Counsel:

*'And would you explain to the Court exactly how
we are to use dreams in this — ah — somewhat
esoteric manner? What are we actually to do with
them different from what has been done hitherto?'
'Perhaps it is not a question of doing anything
different with dreams. Perhaps the secret is to let
dreams do something to you.'
'Very interesting, very interesting. And now pray
tell the Court what do dreams, if you let them,
do to you?'
'They bring you something from afar.'*

This indeed is the unregarded gift of the dreaming mind. Supposing space-men brought back from some remote, inhospitable star — as in fact they may — an organic form, alien, unidentifiable, but undisputably *alive.* With what care, what respect, what passionate interest we would regard it! What infinite possibilities it would raise of a life different in essence, altogether other than our own!

A dream is nothing less than this. It is evidence from another kind of world, proof of another mode of apprehending. Its brilliant combinations of imagery, impossible to the waking mind, involve an ultra-human chemistry of thought. Unlike the heaven of the orthodox and the other-worlds of the sects, with their all-too-human attributes of wish-fulfillment, the dream-world answers neither our hopes nor our fears. The dream-world has the inimitable stamp of *strangeness.*

So alien to us is this farther shore of being to which we are carried in our dreams that we know at once we cannot live there — at least not without losing touch with all the values, and even the meaning, of ordinary life. Only the child and the simple-minded are free to wander, hand in hand, into and out of that fantastic world. For the rest of mankind the invisible prison of everyday has closed around us, leaving open only the narrow window-chink of dreaming.

But this chink is an escape-route of the highest importance. For the dream-world that lies beyond it is the regularly renewed proof that there *is* a farther shore: a secret, private proof, it is true — but everybody's secret, since everybody dreams. This, indeed, is the chief attribute of the dreaming mind: that it makes available to all men everywhere a direct experience, needing no philosophic acrobatics for its acceptance, of that maybe immortal part of us that bursts nightly through the barriers of time and space. To use again the image of the Chalice and the Faces, the dream brings to Chalice-landers authentic news of Face-land.

Even so, as we can gain no more than brief glimpses of the dream-world, of what use can this be to us? Answering that question as it deserves would fill volumes. To accept that every human being has within him an instrument which breaks up the conventional patterns of human perception, disclosing a world outside the range of logic and linear time — is a momentous step. The rules of logic and of cause-and-effect are not invalidated thereby, but they are instantly relativised. Here at last are opposite truths to set beside their truths, binocular vision replaces the one-eyed view of life, 'the doors of perception are opened', and all things are revealed as they are, open-ended and infinite.

How can we learn to use this instrument? How learn to see the intimations of the dreaming mind in an other than merely practical or therapeutic way? The key lies in this: whereas the waking mind looks out, like a

watchman on a tower, at the world of objects, the
dreaming mind stations itself simultaneously both outside and inside all three — the object, the watchman, and
his tower. Such a standpoint lies, of course, beyond our
present comprehension, yet we should remember that
the physicists have already found a name that could
serve for it: the *'absolute elsewhere.'*

The logical waking mind recoils from so monstrous a
paradox, and hastens to bring the images of dreams into
intelligible relationship with what it already understands,
thereby missing the narrow window-chink through which
it might have flown — into the future.

Some years ago I had a dream in which a white bird
fell out of the dark night sky at my feet. I picked it up
and saw that it was dead. But round its neck was a slim
silver chain from which there hung a golden key. In my
dream I was filled with excitement: 'There is a key,' I
cried, 'there is a key!'

It could be the key to the real meaning of our dreams.

12

In Praise of Time

It has been said that if all the human beings in the world were to go mad, an event which now perhaps carries a slightly higher degree of probability than it used to, the general lunacy would exhibit two basic forms — schizophrenia and manic-depression.

There is a grain of truth in this absurd and disagreeable fantasy. Anyone who looks honestly enough into himself will recognise either a tendency to find it difficult to experience whole-hearted and lasting attachments to other people, or a tendency to be the helpless prisoner of such attachments. Pushed to its extreme, the first tendency can develop into the frozen isolation of schizophrenia, the second into the swinging terrors of manic-depression.

A curious relationship, not logical but meaningful, exists between these two forms of insanity and two contrasting aspects of Time: Linear and Cyclical. Though every intelligent person accepts both aspects, there is an underlying bias in each of us, often not consciously recognised, in favour of one or the other. Linear time, of course, starts with an immense advantage as the time we have all been taught to believe in and live by. It is, however, a purely human invention. Linear time is something we have thought up for our own convenience — and very convenient it is for everyday purposes. But it is surely worth noting that no other living creature in existence shares our obsession with linear time. Outside the buzzing human brain-box which has conceived this

linear view of time and imposed it with such astonishing success on human behaviour, the whole of living
creation, from single-celled animalcule up to and including man's own organs, his heart and lungs and in-
testines, lies under the undisputed sway of cyclical
time. Even the human brain itself pulses ceaselessly in
cyclical rhythms, disturbances of which are now accepted
as an indication of mental disorder.

Linear time, on the contrary, is devoid of rhythm, has
no shape. It is a mechanical series of countable, separate,
identical moments. On and on and on it runs, an arrow-
straight autobahn leading to an abyss of nothingness. . .
Just this, experienced with an anguished intensity unimaginable by so-called normal minds, is the private hell
in which the schizophrenic is trapped. It is a featureless
hell. 'The horror of my condition', a highly intelligent
recovered schizophrenic once told me, 'was that the
days had no structure, time had no rhythm'.

In agreeable contrast to this, Cyclical time is filled
with meaning, with colour and change and rhythmical
variations. And cyclical time is no mere human
invention. It arises spontaneously out of the natural
rhythms of life — of morning and evening, of the four
seasons and the changes of the moon, of female periodicities and the flow of tides. It is the time to which all
living creatures, including the human race, responded —
until Western man decided to impose his will on the flux
of events and began to throw spanners into the ex-
quisitely functioning inner rhythms of his own body;
and not merely of his own, but also of the helpless
bodies of his cattle and his poultry. Linear thinking has
tempted man into a deliberate dislocation of natural
rhythms.

Considerations of this kind incline some men to believe that linear time is madness, cyclical time sanity.

But there is more to it than this.

Those who, even in the modern world, tend to look on time as essentially cyclical are really admitting that life and its rhythms are stronger than man's will — as in fact they are. But for some minds, especially in the Far East, this admission brings with it a sense of helplessness which is the sinister aspect of cyclical time. Life can then be experienced as movement in a closed circle, always and endlessly returning to its point of origin. Good fortune follows bad, bad fortune follows good, round and round interminably, a clockwork merry-go-round — or sorry-go-round — that can never run down; till at last the heart grows sick of it all, and longs only to be annihilated. This is the time-world of Buddhists and Reincarnationists: the great revolving Wheel of Time from which even death brings no deliverance. Its all-too-predictable rhythms have in this sense a nightmare quality, the circling, claustrophobic misery of exercise in a prison yard. And this is precisely the misery of manic-depression, with its ever-recurring mood-swings from which the sufferer longs so desperately to escape that even suicide begins to turn into a dark temptation. . .

It seems, then, that both the linear and the cyclical views of time can lead in the long run to a desolating nihilism. But I suggest there may be other approaches, as yet almost untried.

*   *   *

This odd connection between our temporal and our mental attitudes reveals how completely we are involved in time. For ordinary purposes, we look on time as something existing apart from ourselves, something we can 'spend' agreeably, or disagreeably, can even 'kill' if we have a mind to. In this sense we have domesticated time, reducing it to a measurable object which we can divide up into years, weeks, hours, minutes. Yet we are also horribly conscious that time is a tiger stalking us along a lonely road, and that sooner or later we shall feel in some shrinking part of our body the rending claws.

But to see time in this way is to treat it as an external and in the last resort a hostile force. We are so appalled by its destructive aspect that we pay little heed to its sustaining quality. It is as if an intelligent fish, say a dolphin — the one creature with a brain as large as man's — were to experience the sea only as a dark and hostile element, bringer of death and oblivion in one form or another to all the fishy world; and to ignore the liberating fact that the sea is also the element that surrounds and sustains him, the element that is his workshop and playground, that gives him room to develop all his fishy potentialities.

This, however, is exactly how we ourselves behave. 'Time', we chant lugubriously on Sunday, 'like an ever-rolling stream bears all its sons away'. 'Ah, fill the cup', we say with a crooked grin on week-days, 'what boots it to repeat how Time is slipping underneath our feet' — and so on and so on. Poets, artists and theologians vie with each other in the effort to bring home to us the dark aspect of Time, the precarious brevity of life, the bleak fact that the paths of glory lead but to the grave.

All true, of course, depressingly true. Nothing reveals human impotence more harshly than the inexorable passing of time. But this is only half the story, only one view of time's Janus-face. To concentrate on it exclusively is no less foolish than to see doors as capable only of closing — of shutting out friends, of closing in prisoners, of barring the way, like Keats' great black door that is 'shut against the sunrise evermore'. Doors can also open, suddenly and invitingly. Time, too,

has this dual power.

Time's chief and amazing attribute, which passes almost unnoticed, is this, that every hour of every day there stretches before me a boundless expanse of *unused time*, of which — unless I am ill or in gaol — I am complete and undisputed master, to employ exactly as I wish. The sheer power inherent in this freedom is intoxicating — when· we remember it, which is seldom. That what I actually do is to clear up the breakfast things, drive the children to school, or catch the 8.15 to the City, is my own affair, my own choice. If I lack the confidence or the ruthlessness or the disregard of consequences to try to hi-jack a plane, or paint a picture, or hit my enemy over the head with an axe and bury him under the floorboards, it is no one else's fault. No one can stop me attempting *anything* in the unused time that lies miraculously open before me. Indeed, every time I open a newspaper I see that someone has actually done some such thing and my compulsive interest in the exploit arises out of the fleeting intuition, 'that could have been me. . .'

We are much more influenced than we suppose by the *image* we have of ourselves. What we privately see ourselves to be, that we are likely to become. This is not to be confused with the carefully edited image of ourselves we present to others. P.R. experts have made us all so keenly aware of this 'image' and its social importance that it has become a cult word. The only image of a man that really matters is the secret one he has of himself. We are not very clear-sighted about this, even if left alone. But we are not left alone. Philosophers and scientists are continually persuading us to accept the idea that we are far less free than we think, that decisions we imagine we have freely made are in fact merely the resultant of forces acting on us from the environment or from the unconscious. This again is depressingly true. But over against it is the other, the paradoxical truth which few pause to consider: that man also stands at every moment of his life, like a child at the sea's edge, facing a limitless ocean of possibility.

Time has another liberating attribute: as the future is filled with infinite potentiality, so the past is endlessly *transformable*. There is a certain kind of thinker who denies this and takes a morose delight in what he considers the iron irreversibility of past events. But the past is never static. Pessimistic Khayyam may tell us that —

> *The moving Finger writes, and having writ*
> *Moves on, nor all your piety and wit*
> *Can ever serve to cancel one half-line,*
> *nor all your tears wash out one word of it*

but we do not have to believe him. There are others, notably Professor F. Kummel, the German philosopher of time, who see with equal certainty that past events, of personal as of world history, are in constant movement and impossible to hold in a steady perspective; like distant mountains whose contours and colours continuously melt and change in the lengthening shadows of a summer evening.

*   *   *

To have a rich and living response to time's meaning, we must become capable of seeing for what they are the ever-changing masks which hide the unknowable face of time. We must not allow ourselves to be argued into accepting any one of these masks — linear or cyclical, sustaining or destructive, transformable or irreversible — as preferable to any other. (We are in good company. Kant declared that he could prove irrefutably that time *had* a beginning — and that it had *not*). But it is a difficult attitude to maintain. For man the inveterate image-maker feels a compulsive urge to find an image for time, and is then seduced, like Aaron's Israelites with their Golden Calf, by the image he has himself created.

Yet it is probably necessary to make room for this image-making propensity in man. The question is, can an image be found which, like time itself, defies a final analysis? Kummel has attempted to do just this, in the image of an *open circle*. 'Man is contained', he says, 'in an open circle of time in which the past never assumes a final shape and the future never shuts its doors'. This is superb as a concept, but unsatisfactory as an image. A circle is by definition a perfect figure, without beginning or end, so that an 'open circle' is impossible to visualise. But there does exist an image, not merely visual but concrete and factual, that is capable of expressing the paradox of an 'open circle'. *The spiral is such an image.* A spiral is in itself a visual paradox. Seen from the side, it consists of a wavy line which we know only requires sufficient tension at each end to draw it into a straight one. Seen from vertically above, a spiral consists of a circle which appears to be a closed and perfect figure, though we know in fact it is open. To ask which of these two figures is the true image of time is to share the mental equipment of a man who asks, on being shown two projections of a house, one in elevation and one in plan, 'Ah, but which is the *real* house?'

The figure of a spiral is no casual choice. Nature itself is greatly taken with spirals, and plays unending variations on this single theme, from the helical homes of snails and a thousand sea-creatures, the spiralling horns of a multitude of animals, the coiled cochlear organs of human ears, up to the monstrous and menacing spirals of whirlpools, water-spouts and tornadoes. Working at the opposite end of the scale, two physicists, Watson and Crick, won the Nobel Prize in 1962 for their demonstration that the basic DNA molecule, which holds the secret of the genes, has the structure of a double spiral. In short, there is more to the spiral in every sense than meets the eye.

No image of the mystery of time can be wholly satisfactory. The image of the spiral can at least contain and express the liberating paradox of a time-world that is at the same moment complete — and open-ended.

13

Psyche Assailed

The contemporary vogue for psychology has progressively devalued the word *psyche* until everybody thinks they know what it means. 'Psyche? Why, it just means Mind.' They don't go on to ask themselves what Mind means. If pressed they would probably say that mind means the sum of mental processes or mechanisms.

In Greek the word psyche means two things: breath, soul, spirit, and — a butterfly. Something at once timeless as the spirit, yet wayward and ephemeral as a Swallow-tail: a perfect paradox. And paradox alone can contain its total meaning.

What is the psyche? As befits so great a mystery, it is hard to tell. It is that in us which is born of the encounter of opposites, which honours the unknown equally with the known, the darkness equally with the light; it is that in us which lies beyond defining, which points always beyond itself, leaving the world open-ended. Spontaneous, unpredictable, free, its very existence is a challenge to logical thought, the glitter of an executioner's axe to every strutting orthodoxy. The psyche is beautiful and dangerous.

Whenever and wherever the psyche appears in its wholeness, it is therefore immediately attacked. 'The individual psyche is a snare,' thunders the Church, 'and will lead you fatally astray. Put your faith in Authority!' 'The psyche is nothing but infantile sexuality, nothing but the will-to-power,' Freud and Adler confidentially assure us in the twilight of the consulting-room. 'The psyche is a chimaera! It does not exist!' scream the Behaviourists.

These last are indeed three deadly threats to the life of the psyche, coming as they do from those who ought to be its friends. All three provide rational explanations for the disturbing behaviour of the psyche, and the world is foolishly grateful for this. For the one thing Everyman craves beyond all else is a ready-made, foolproof, unsinkable philosophy which he can slip on like a cork waist-coat, and then get on with everyday life.

Freud, Adler and the Behaviourists each have a model of this desirable garment in stock. And there is no doubt that it gives its wearers an enviable sense of security. But to the psyche it is an intolerable strait-jacket, more strictly mechanistic than modern physicists dare to be, preventing all movements but those permitted by these presumptuous tailors. The psyche, like Truth, is comfortable only when naked — as Jaspers and Jung almost alone among leaders of psychology have had the wit to recognise.

What is the cause of this hostility that confronts the psyche from so many influential quarters? Could it be that the psyche, itself the essence of the paradoxical, sees all things in the light of paradox, thereby challenging the stubborn delusion of mankind that somewhere, somewhen, a final answer can be found to the riddle of existence? Two facts, at least, are undeniable: that from time to time through human history the psyche has given birth to an idea of explosive and revolutionary force; and that the established orders have instantly and automatically ranged themselves in opposition.

Their technique is unvarying. As soon as a major threat to an orthodoxy appears, a quiet attempt is set in motion to murder the Idea in its cradle before the world even knows that it has been born: what might be called the Herod reaction. When this fails — as it must, since such ideas are immortal — subtle temptations are offered to lure it from its purpose. When these are rejected and the Idea begins to gain ground, skilled arguments laced with ridicule are employed to discredit it. Finally just when the Idea, having survived these attacks, seems at last to have a chance of universal acceptance, there appears spontaneously — as if created by the desperate need of the endangered power-system — the man of fatal genius: the Interpreter.

The historic role of the Interpreter is to transmute the revolutionary Idea into a form that can peacefully co-exist with established values. A man of genius is required because the transmutation must be intellectually impeccable. Poor Everyman feels vaguely cheated by this *tour de force*, but can do nothing effective about it, for the subtle modifications have first been carried out at a level of genius far above his head, then skilfully elaborated, and finally presented to him with all the persuasive force at the disposal of a highly organised propaganda machine.

Only rarely does the psyche give birth to such world-transforming ideas — barely half a dozen times in the whole of human history. The Interpreter is therefore an exceptional phenomenon. But in spite of the rarity of his appearance on the world-stage, he and his kind are a fascinating group for study. Lonely geniuses they are, usually misunderstood; sometimes, like Paul, martyred by the temporal powers they serve. They have some features in common with the Juggler of the Tarot Pack —shrewd, brilliant, dextrous like him, but also gifted with his disturbing numinous power.

It is difficult to say whether the Interpreter does more harm than good — so much depends on the point of view. Jacob, who tricked his aged father Isaac into giving the eldest son's blessing to him instead of to his brother Esau, was a crude prototype of the Interpreter. It was an ugly trick. But by its means Jacob created a nation which has defied to this day all attempts to destroy it. He was able to do so because of his blazing certainty that he had been divinely appointed for this purpose.

Here is the key to the Interpreter's success. He is passionately sincere, and the services he renders to the temporal power are entirely unconscious. His opportune arrival on the scene is one of those coincidences that tease the mind with the hint of a hidden meaning. The temporal power never chooses the Interpreter. Indeed, commonly it mistakes him at first for an enemy. Neither does he espouse the cause of the temporal power. He flames into existence motivated solely by an unconquerable inner conviction — and arrives in the nick of time. He sees himself as a bold innovator and iconoclast — and is in fact the unconscious saviour of the status quo. The Western world has produced two major figures of this type: Paul and Freud.

The central teaching of Jesus, as defined in the Sermon on the Mount, is one of the most paradoxical and revolutionary religious manifestoes that have ever been offered to the world. 'Blessed are the poor, blessed are the meek, blessed are they who are persecuted —' are not principles likely to be welcomed by the holders of power. From their own point of view Provincial Governor and High Priest alike were quite justified in feeling alarm. Jesus, as they knew from earlier secret police reports, came from a dangerously subversive family. Even before he was born his mother had been heard to burst into a song which was nothing short of incitement to anarchy. There it was, in the official files:

'My soul doth magnify the Lord,' sang the Virgin Mary,
'For he hath regarded the low estate of his hand-
maiden . . .
He hath shown strength with his arm: he hath
scattered the proud in the imagination of their
hearts.
He hath put down the mighty from their seats, and
exalted them of low degree.
He hath filled the hungry with good things; and the
rich he hath sent empty away.'

A deplorable song. Obviously such doctrines could never be tolerated in a well-ordered society. From birth the life of Jesus was in constant danger, and his eventual judicial murder was a foregone conclusion. But to their dismay the authorities found that the Christian Idea survived the removal of its Founder in spite of, and in part because of, unabated persecution. The classic conditions had now been constellated in which an Interpreter of genius was urgently required. As always, the need was miraculously met. Paul was the unwitting answer to the Establishment's prayer.

By combining a passionate zeal for the Founder of Christianity and the imaginative vigour of a great poet, with a soldierly determination to achieve the triumph of Christianity throughout the world, Paul did a real service for the secular powers. For it became possible eventually to trim Pauline Christianity to fit the needs of a militaristic state religion. The original Christian message could never have been so trimmed.

Far from having the socially disruptive effect of the original teaching of Jesus, which had so disquieted Government circles and so infuriated the priest-hood, Pauline Christianity had the makings, though at first unrecognised, of a *socially manageable* religion. The administrative flair and masculine drive of Paul, his tireless setting-up of orderly Christian centres, his curt bringing-to-heel of disobedient minorities, his strict and unforgiving moral principles, swiftly transformed the scattered revolutionary bands of early Christians into a solid, well-knit religious organisation with what the stockbrokers call excellent growth prospects.

It took time, of course. But after three centuries of gradually waning persecution this amended Christianity of Paul began to fit surprisingly neatly into the power-structure of the Roman Empire. So neatly and supportively that around A.D. 415 we find a leading Father of the early Church, St. Augustine, suavely defending the principle of slavery, and setting up the famous four pillars of social security in human affairs. How sweet the names of 'Pax, Ordo, Lex, Societas' sound in the Establishment ear!

The fact that the Romans killed Paul for his pains is one of the ironies of history. They mistook him for an enemy — the occupational hazard of an Interpreter — and although the precise form of his martyrdom is still uncertain, it is believed that Nero fed him to the lions. Yet Paul unwittingly worked well for Rome, as later events were to prove. In A.D. 312 Emperor Constantine the Great, when changing the state religion from the martial creed of Mithraism to Christianity, is reported to have declared that he could see remarkably few points of difference between the two religions.

The Interpreter's role is always equivocal. Who can say if Paul did ill or well? Like his ancestor Jacob he undoubtedly made possible the founding of a politically powerful religious force. For centuries the Church of Rome has been, and remains, a pervasive influence in human affairs. But Paul's achievement is not, of course, to everyone's taste. *C'est magnifique, mais —*

* * *

The Western world had to wait a long while for the appearance of an Interpreter of comparable stature to Paul. Predictably so, since such a figure could be evoked only by an equally basic threat to the temporal powers. In 1832 such a threat appeared: at first just a little cloud in the nineteenth century sky, 'no bigger than a man's hand.' But that small cloud presaged a storm in the mind of man after which nothing can ever be quite the same again.

In that year a poet and novelist called C. Nodier published his views on the vital part played in human life by sleep, dreams and what was then the little-known concept of the unconscious mind. His views were dangerously disruptive to the social fabric of his day. 'Since there are two powers in man, or if one may so express it, two spirits which rule him [the imaginative and creative forces of the dreaming mind and the positivist principles of waking] . . . which is the better of the two states? If I dare to state my opinion, since man cannot escape . . . the obligation of accepting and fulfilling the conditions of his double nature, *both are impossible in an exclusive application.* In a country where the positive principle alone claims to reign over all opinions, there is nothing left to do but to renounce the name of man and retire to the woods . . . for such a society does not deserve any other farewell.'

Here spoke out a true and early champion of the psyche: to be followed shortly by the whole school of Romantic writers, proclaiming — but, alas, absurdly overemphasising — the paramount importance of the world of the Unconscious. As mere exponents of a particular school of literature, however, their views could be safely ignored in the corridors of power — and were.

Exactly thirty years later there appeared a more formidable champion of the revolutionary potential of the psyche. The world-famous *Journal* of Amiel, the Swiss philosopher, contains the following entry, dated 9th August 1862: 'The wise part of us . . . is that which is unconscious of itself; and what is most reasonable in man are those elements in him which do not reason. Instinct, nature, a divine and impersonal activity, heal in us the wounds made by our own follies . . . The essential, material basis of our conscious life is therefore that unconscious life which we perceive no more than the outer hemisphere of the moon perceives the earth, while all the time indissolubly and eternally bound to it.'

Some thirty years later still the first real threat to social stability, arising out of a growing recognition of the numinous power of the psyche, was expressed in words which rolled and echoed like thunder around the world. Nietzsche's call to man to surpass himself, to look beyond the petty limits of the conscious mind, his Promethean cry that the time was ripe for 'the transvaluation of all values,' were ideas that just possibly could have transformed the Western world: they could not be left unanswered. Nietzsche's eventual lapse into lunacy was a lucky windfall for power-systems everywhere; nevertheless the challenge he had thrown down had to be met.

'Safer' views of the psyche had of course long been current in medical and philosophic circles, and many writers had already attempted to explain the disconcerting behaviour of the psyche on strictly rational grounds. But none had, like Nietzsche, so caught the world's attention.

111

Certainly for the majority of citizens the solid edifice of nineteenth century social values stood firm as ever; but the holders of power were disturbed. They had become aware that the very foundations of their system were being steadily eroded by dark invisible currents from the unconscious. Sniffing the air like blood-hounds, their twitching nostrils detected a whiff of revolution, a unique, non-political kind of revolution, beginning secretly in the individual human heart — and all the more dangerous for that. Here was a psychic force, they recognised, that might suddenly become incandescent in the mind, radiating outward with such nuclear and apocalyptic power that everything would be changed; the first might all too easily find itself last, and the last first. Plainly, this could not be allowed . . . Once more, an Interpreter of genius was urgently required.

Freud was the perfect antidote to this yeasty ferment in the mind of man. True to the historical destiny of an Interpreter, his role was at first unrecognised and he was savagely attacked on all sides. Freud was prepared for this. He saw himself as a fearless innovator and, like Paul, was reconciled in advance to martyrdom. With his epoch-making book *The Interpretation of Dreams*, published in 1900, he burst upon the world filled with a flaming certainty that he had solved the frightening enigma of the psyche. And in one sense he was justified. Without his discoveries a vital factor in man would have remained in the shadows — who knows for how long? He forced the entire world to pay attention to the unexplored territory of the unconscious; and this is his immortal achievement.

But, again like Paul, he unwittingly betrayed the spirit of the cause he championed. His betrayal stemmed from the fact that, until he found a rational technique for controlling it, Freud himself was mortally afraid of the raw, living substance of the unconscious. Once, during an historic argument with Jung he exclaimed with great emotion — 'My dear Jung, promise me never to abandon the sexual theory. That is the most essential thing of all. You see, we must make a dogma of it, an unshakeable bulwark.' In some astonishment Jung asked him 'A bulwark against what?' To which he replied, 'against the black mud tide of occultism.' To vary his metaphor, Freud saw the unconscious as a wild beast too dangerous to approach till it had been tamed. Only after skilful doctoring was he able to perform the crowd-pulling feat of thrusting his head, like a lion-tamer, into the gaping mouth of the unconscious and withdrawing it unharmed.

Freud knew himself to be the loyal servant of Science — the curiously arrogant science of his day — and his whole aim was to bring to what he regarded as the dark, unruly impulses of the psyche the blessing of a rational approach. Armed with the nineteenth century scientific spirit he strode into the savage and beautiful country of the Unconscious with all the quiet confidence of a God-fearing explorer stepping into a jungle; and with the same tragically misplaced certainty that he was bringing a shining and superior ethos into a benighted land.

The simile is apt. For precisely the same unintended injury was inflicted on the inner world by the Freudian invader as was suffered by the world of the dark-skinned races through the invaders from Europe. The misapprehension of the autonomous, atemporal, amoral values of the inner world, the arrogant nineteenth century conviction that the logical principles of the conscious mind could be strictly applied in explanation of inner world events — this was the cardinal Freudian error. The equally gross undervaluation of the meanings to be found in the cultures of dark-skinned races, the bland assurance that

European standards and beliefs would be of inestimable value to them was, in exact parallel, the cardinal error of nineteenth century colonists. As might be expected the results are similar in both cases; but only the former need be followed here.

Freud is a giant and fateful figure in the development of Western thought. His concept of the dark regions of the Unconscious as backward areas to be reclaimed and re-educated by the colonising vigour of the scientific mind has now become part of the mental background of Western Everyman. The details of the argument soar far above Everyman's head, but he feels confident that he has grasped the general idea. The age-old humbling sense of things unknowable, of forces for ever beyond man's control, has been lifted from him. Much remains, he knows, to be explained, much remains that he personally will never be able to explain; but he has the comfortable feeling that now there are men in the world who can and will undertake this task. The fact that the top scientists of the twentieth century make no such claim has almost escaped his notice. As far as Everyman is concerned, the burden of the mystery has been taken over by the experts. They may quarrel and dispute, as egg-heads do, over details; they may raise points about which even he, as far as he can follow them, feels a bit dubious; and at all times he considers himself fully entitled to make fun of them.

Behind all this, however, he feels vaguely reassured. Now at last there is, he understands, 'a Science of the Mind.' Psyche, the immortal butterfly has been captured and lies safely pinned down on an entomologist's tray. It can only be a matter of time before her ultimate secrets are ferreted out by the professors, and neatly recorded. The Final Answer is on the way, and Everyman can now get on without misgiving with the dear banalities of everyday life. Which is exactly what the power-systems of the world would like him to do.

It was a near thing, though. Psychoanalytic theory and practice were only just in time to deflect into medical and therapeutic channels what might have proved an apocalyptic expansion of spiritual values in human consciousness. Once again the Interpreter has apparently done a good job.

But has he? This time there was a major flaw in the performance as compared with Paul's. The re-alignment of Christianity orchestrated by Paul gave the guardians of social security a very long breathing-space; but the respite provided by Freud has been brief indeed. His carefully planned control of the forces of the unconscious by means of the 'unshakeable bulwark' of the pan-sexual theory has proved inadequate. His attempt to tone down the psyche into a well-behaved speciality of medicine labelled Psychoanalysis has signally failed. The genie is out of the bottle and nothing will ever persuade it to go back again. It may be that Freud will be one day remembered as the last of the great Interpreters, the one whose over-confidence uncorked the bottle and allowed the beautiful and dangerous psyche to escape.

14

Chaos and Order

Intoxicated by its new-found freedom, resentful at the abortive Freudian attempt to clip its wings, the psyche is now roaming the contemporary scene in a particularly ugly mood, apparently intent on nothing less than the immediate overthrow of all traditional values and the undermining of the four great Augustinian pillars on which organised society rests. To the holders of temporal power the current behaviour of the liberated psyche more than justifies the hostility they have always shown towards it. In their eyes the psyche now appears as a purely destructive force, openly aiming to involve the whole world in a kind of experimental chaos of quarrelling factions.

In a sense this is true. If there is one thing that distinguishes the contemporary scene from any other, it is the popularity of protest. Suddenly everyone everywhere is protesting against something — even if a minority are only protesting against those who protest. A hideous rash of protest and counter-protest is flaring like a Scarlet Fever across the suffering face of the world. What is the meaning of this ugly symptom? What will be the course of the disease?

The outcome must be doubtful, but the meaning is surely plain. Such violent reactions occur only when both sides believe in their hearts that their deepest values, the ones they live by, are threatened. And this is no illusion. Between Face-lander and Chalice-lander, as we have seen, no compromise can exist, for it is impossible to see both Chalice and Faces at the same time. On the level at which such a struggle is conducted, which is the level of all the rancorous quarrels of our time — black against white, youth against age, Licence against Authority, Peace-at-any-price against War-to-end-war — the chimaera of total defeat or total victory is the only solution acceptable to either side. And in all these quarrels the confrontation of forces is in the final analysis the same, and is basic. Dionysian and Apollonian challenge each other as never before. The two aspects of mind, Unconscious and Conscious, have been suddenly polarised by the fateful genius of Freud.

There can be little doubt that the current is now floating strongly in favour of the forces of the Unconscious. These forces are rising all round us to the surface of life, while our conscious values are being increasingly submerged. And the process is by no means completed. We are on our way to wilder shores than any we have yet visited. To some this state of affairs feels like the dawning of a new era, a time in which it is 'bliss to be alive'; to others it appears as an apparently deliberate movement towards chaos, towards the non-sequitur, towards the experiencing of life as a demonstration of the Sartrian Absurd. For a third group, which includes the majority of us, it is frighteningly confusing. Movements towards the irrational have, of course, often occurred before, as with the Dadaists or the Surrealists; but these were confined to small intellectual and artistic coteries. Today this movement has a world-wide momentum. It expresses the enthusiastic and belligerent convictions of millions.

Like it or not, therefore, we have to react in some way to what is happening; and we appear to be inescapably faced with the decision: *for or against*. The struggle between *for* and *against* has been described in a Zen

Buddhist poem as the mind's worst disease. Certainly in our present situation it can offer no solution. But there is a time-honoured way out of all such dilemmas: to begin the search for a reconciling principle. As always, it is to be looked for in some neglected corner. For as Simone Weil has said, that which belongs to a new order can appear in the old order only in the guise of something infinitely small. Or as Nietzsche unforgettably put it — 'Thoughts that come on dove's feet control the world.' In our day this quietly emergent principle, I am going to suggest in the chapter following, is *Rhythm*. In the sense in which I use the term, Rhythm is the concern at present of a mere handful of physiologists and ecologists; but this very fact fulfills, as we have seen, one of the conditions for a new point of departure.

*　　*　　*

To look first at the chaotic side of contemporary society: as we all know, there is evidence of a fundamental change of attitude towards authority and leadership among young people everywhere. And when I speak of youth and young people I am not referring exclusively to chronological age, but to a specific mental attitude towards events; many people are born middle-aged. At this moment in history the youthful part of the human race is preparing not merely to change its leaders — which would be nothing new — but to change its *type* of leader. In the current youthful concept of leadership the emphasis is now falling less on high I.Q. and organising genuis, and more on purely emotional qualities. And incidentally in this change of emphasis the computer, with its almost incredible powers, is playing an unnoticed but important part. Human intelligence is no longer the unique and irreplaceable instrument it has always been till now. Much of the brain's expertise has been successfully mechanised. To youth, the computer is one of the new brooms with which the ancient rule of the Establishment can be largely swept aside. As usual, youth is here exaggerating; but it has a point.

To the further question of what *kind* of emotional qualities the new type of leader should possess, two apparently opposing answers are emerging. The 'irresistible' torrent of youth meeting the 'immovable' square rock of traditional values, has split into two antithetical streams, one flowing towards liberation by violence, the other towards liberation through love. In many cases the individual adolescent has himself split on this rock, half of him going one way and half the other. This confuses the issue both for himself and others.

But the two streams are nevertheless discernible and separable. They make for entirely opposite goals: one towards the mirage of absolute revolutionary power, the other towards a warm but woolly idealism. They have profoundly different leaders — Ché Guevara, Mao, Cohn-Bendit and their like — who could be described as the Violent Heroes, as against what could be called the Singing Heroes, such bizarre yet undeniably charismatic figures as Mick Jagger, Elton John, and in their day, the Beatles. It should be noted that each one of these folk-heroes could draw far larger crowds of partisans than any Prime Minister or President. Whatever 'explanations' are offered, this constitutes an empirical fact and may not be shrugged off.

We are apt to fear the Violent Heroes, and smile at the Singing Heroes. In this we are wrong. The Violent Heroes and the Singing Heroes are among the mythic figures of today — and *all* mythic figures are daimonic, and fateful. In the last resort the Singing Heroes are as ruthless in pursuit of their ideals as the others. They both spell the destruction of traditional values, the breaking of a mould. It may, or may not, be that the destruction is timely, that the mould deserves to be broken. Be that as it may, the very appearance on the historical plane of such mythic figures marks, in fact, the end of an epoch. It is not a question of 'coming to terms with them', or of 'learning to live with them'. The figures of myth cannot be lived with. They cannot be condescendingly 'understood'. They are the fantastic high priests of transition. Their function is to bring about the transvaluation of all values, as Nietzsche foresaw. They can be resisted, perhaps must be resisted, to make the change less sudden and catastrophic. But change will come. I suggest we are living through a large-scale death and re-birth experience, a re-enactment in psychological terms of the primordial myth of the Great Flood. Our generation has been overtaken by giant birth-pangs, and has no certainty of what it is about to bring into the world: smiling infant — or misshapen anencephalic monster.

But however uncertain we may be of our immediate destiny, of one thing at least we can be sure: we are being torn from our ancient moorings. The hard edges of our world are everywhere dissolving, as in a dream, or a Dali landscape. Our age is in one sense an age of reckless Carnival. As happened more than once in mediaeval times, we have aroused the sleeping forces of Carnival — giant figures that we cannot control or contain. The order-loving part of the mind looks on appalled as these grotesque avatars, that belong to the fantasy life of the deep unconscious, shoulder their way into the everyday world, jostling us in the broad noon-day streets, bullying us in the daily papers, gesturing at us from the T.V. screen . . . It is the world of myth, which we have too long repudiated, returning upon us in irresistible strength. We are being swept, some shivering with dismay, some with exaltation, into the mythic style of life.

In such vertiginous times it is not surprising that the quietist philosophies of the Far East have suddenly become popular in the Western world. Historically, Taoism in China, Buddhism in India took root in two lands where life for more than forty centuries was fantastically precarious. In both countries petty wars, rebellions and invasions were continuous, starvation following droughts and floods claimed thousands of lives each year, Government corruption and avarice allowed no one to feel secure, and the powers and punishments of the rulers were cruel and capricious. In such desperate conditions, the saffron-robed Buddhist and the Taoist 'mountain man', standing serene and untouched above the general confusion and violence, must have seemed figures from an ideal world quietly offering, without insistence, the only possible means of escape.

No wonder that these two figures, irrelevant as they may appear to the contemporary scene, exert a powerful attraction today in the Western world. For it is only in an atmosphere of multifarious conflict and bitter distrust, with mini-wars breaking out everywhere, so heated and so numerous as to become meaningless: only then does the human mind grow sufficiently sick of its own futile fantasies of victory that it reaches out with the courage of despair for its equally fantasied opposite, a state of ineffable peace and detachment. The Warrior Victor and the Illumined Philosopher are both fantasy-figures — considered as realisable human beings. But here lies the paradox. For they both co-exist as potentialities within the human soul. The real value of an extreme situation is that it constellates its opposite in the psyche, and enables a man to become aware of the dangerous polarities in his own and other people's natures. Only the spirit of paradox is able to contain these opposites and so avoid the tragedy of taking sides.

How then shall we adjust to this state of affairs — those of us who try to keep our heads and hearts above the purely controversial level? Merely to jump on to the band-waggon of instant chaos is no answer. Merely to resist change, in favour of the old order is not enough. To compromise is to evade the issue. In such an impasse there is but one solution: *we must find a new point of departure.*

The discovery and fostering of this growing-point is the prime task for the creative minds of today. I suggest that this growing-point has already appeared and is to be found in the unobtrusive but all-pervasive phenomenon of *Rhythm.*

15

Rhythm

Do not be misled by the definition you will find in the dictionary. Rhythm is a mystery. It is the invisible wave on which Life itself is carried. Rhythm is also the antidote to the slow poison of linear time. The action of a pendulum clock in a silent room has two meanings: the minute-hand tells us that life is bleeding to death, drop by regular drop, from the irrecoverable wound of Time; and the pendulum tells us that life and death, life and death, are in perfect and timeless equilibrium. The meaning of rhythm is not definable by any human agency, because it surrounds and invades and contains us.

Nearly two hundred years ago there was a poet who was aware of the centrality and ubiquity of rhythm. In one of his beautiful 'Hymns to the Night' Novalis had this to say about it: 'Seasons, times of the day, lives and destinies, are all, strikingly enough, thoroughly rhythmical, metrical, according to a beat. In all trades and arts, in all machines, in organic bodies, in our daily functions, everywhere: rhythm, metre, beat, melody. Anything we do with a certain skill we do rhythmically without being aware of it. Rhythm is found everywhere. There must be more to this . . .' There is, indeed.

Paradoxically, the *perception* of rhythm is a uniquely human achievement. All existence *illustrates* rhythm; we alone *perceive* it. But the capacity to perceive something is not identical with the capacity to define it. And in truth the most we can do with rhythm is to observe its effects and tune ourselves in to its invisible power.

Let us observe its effects.

To begin, then, with ourselves, the life of the human body is an intricate complex of inter-relating rhythms: waking and sleeping, action and rest, feeding and evacuation, the delicate Berger rhythms of the brain, menstrual cycles, mood-swings — which in cases of manic-depression are sometimes as rhythmical as the phases of the moon, or of the seasons; gastric and duodenal ulcers, which in some people erupt at regular intervals of time. There are also forms of neuritic pain which occur for some completely unexplained reason at exactly the same hour of each day.

These are matters of common experience. But scientific research, aided by computering techniques, is almost daily disclosing more subtle rhythmical manifestations in man: diurnal cycles in body-temperature, regular sequences of dream-activity, electrical cycles in heart and lungs and liver, hormonal changes running parallel to changes in the seasons — these and many other human rhythms are now coming into view. Rhythms, in fact, insinuate themselves into every organ of the body, and even into all its cells. There is evidence that there is more than one so-called 'biological clock' in each single cell of every living organism. With one striking exception, which we will come to in a moment.

The most widespread of all the rhythms that we know of as yet, is that related to the alternations of day and night. Professor Franz Halberg, one of the most distinguished researchers in this field, has coined for it the delightful word 'circadian' — meaning 'about a day'. The circadian type of rhythm is found in every animal and plant, even in a blind animal, and in a plant that is kept in continual darkness. This leads to the startling conclusion that, running through almost every species of living organisms is a dim *awareness of cyclical time,* due to this indwelling circadian rhythm.

One curious and ominous exception to this is found in the life-pattern of bacteria and viruses. According to Karl Hamner, Professor of Botany in the University of California, bacteria and viruses possess neither rhythms nor a' time-sense comparable to that of higher organisms. Their blind, formless, unrhythmical mode of growth occurs elsewhere, I personally venture to believe, only in that other basic enemy of life, the cancer-cell. There could, I suppose, be a connection here — but that is another matter.

The questions raised by these recent researches are beginning to excite scientific attention, and a growing amount of work is now being carried out on human and animal rhythms by ecologists and biologists, notably in America, France, England and Germany. Strange facts have already emerged — as that the killing power of insecticides depends on the hour of administration; that resistance to toxic organisms in small animals varies considerably according to the time of day at which infection occurs; and that in human beings operative risks are greater at one time of day than another. Dr. Alain Reinberg of France believes the day not far distant when there will be a recognised science of what he calls 'temporal therapeutics', correlating human rhythms with medical treatment.

Some tentative steps in this direction have already been taken. That powerful and original thinker Preston Harold, already quoted in Chapter VIII, has put forward the at first sight bizarre suggestion, in relation to the New Testament miracles of the raisings of the apparently dead, that rhythmical sonic waves may be involved; an idea which gives us what may be our first glimpse of an as yet undreamed of region of human consciousness.

Harold's contention is that the miracles of Jesus were

achieved through his incomparable hypnotic powers. Exceptional Being that he was, Jesus was able usually to dispense with hypnotic preliminaries, though it is recorded that occasionally (notably in making a paste of spittle and dust and laying it on a blind man's eyes) he used what could be regarded as a technique of this kind. Normally, however, he could rely on the immediate effect of his voice and gestures, endowed with — who can now tell? — what compelling qualities of rhythm, to penetrate like a laser ray to the depths of the defeated psyche and accomplish the miracle of reanimation.

Bold as this concept may be, it is in harmony with several current lines of investigation. For instance, a Swiss general practitioner, Hans Jenny, has recently demonstrated in London and elsewhere a series of experiments revealing the power of sonic waves to reorganise certain forms of matter in rhythmic patterns of great beauty. The implications of this are far-reaching, and are as yet almost unexplored.

A more clinical approach to the untapped potential of sonic waves appeared recently in *The Lancet,* a leading British medical journal, which printed a report on 'three patients who had sustained primary brain damage, and were comatose for 63, 14 and 13 days respectively. *The recovery of each coincided with the commencement of continuous auditory stimulation.* Radio One (B.B.C. popular music programme) was relayed to each patient through earphones for 10 hours a day.' A full case-history of each case was given in the report. The doctor concerned cautiously observed that 'the association between auditory stimulation and recovery may be entirely fictitious.' He thought, however, that there was a connection, since in the normal way 'patients in coma receive little stimulation of their special senses. Relatives who visit comatose patients sit mute beside them, too embarrassed to talk.' He suggested that 'visitors should be encouraged to speak at length to unconscious patients, and that continuous Radio One therapy should be undertaken.' It is perhaps a pity that pop music should be the recommended sonic waves to be employed. One might prefer to be resuscitated by the Seventh Symphony — but that is hardly the point!

These experiments are of particular interest to me because, years before this report appeared, in the two or three instances where I have found patients in a desperate strait — where medical science seemed to have shot its bolt — I have by some almost unconscious compulsion sent nurses and others out of the room, taken the patient in my arms and whispered in their ear a few words — 'Don't be afraid. I will bring you back. I am going to make you well', or some such thing. I don't think it mattered what I said. The impact was accomplished by the rhythmic patterns of sound and gesture. One woman who was in a deep bromide coma I kissed on the cheek, though she was a complete stranger to me. Most 'unprofessional', I suppose, but I knew that I had to do just this. It may be worth recording that in each case, in spite of being apparently comatose, they had a curiously clear recollection of what I said and did. And they all three 'came back'.

But perhaps they would have, anyway. Who can say?

What could be called this tuning-in process is a vital part of the procedure in hypnosis. The faintly absurd preliminaries of hypnotic induction — the swinging watch-chain, the ticking metronome, the sing-song repetitive phrases of the hypnotist — all these are attempts to establish a shared rhythm between patient and operator. The patient is lulled and caressed and carried unresistingly along on regular waves of sight or sound. The same process is part of the hypnotic effect of poetry, of music — and of waterfalls.

All these lines of thought and research are based on the idea that there exists in living tissue some kind of indwelling and independent timing system. This is remarkable enough, but evidence is accumulating that an even more unlikely factor must be taken into account. Further investigation into these 'biological clocks' discloses, in the words of Frank A. Brown, Morison Professor of Biology at Northwestern University, Illinois, that the clocks are 'themselves probably timed by subtle pervasive variations in the earth's atmosphere effected by the relative movements of the earth, sun and moon'. Cosmic radiations, in short, may be involved.

This was altogether too much for the scientific Establishment. Hardly had it swallowed, with considerable reluctance, the now incontrovertible fact of indwelling biological clocks in all living tissues, than it was asked to accept the possibility of these clocks being at least partly controlled by rhythmic radiations from the stars and planets.

One can sympathise with the acute discomfort of responsible scientists who find the investigations of some of their colleagues bringing them suddenly into close proximity with the catch-penny perpetrators of 'The Stars Foretell' columns in the daily papers. In fact their discomfort was such that the scientific world, with only a few exceptions, has greeted the theory with scorn and incredulity. This was to be expected. Blind Man's Bluff is still the spontaneous reaction of the Authorities to the appearance of a subversive idea.

On this occasion the reaction is understandable, and may even be valuable. Too ready an acceptance could create an uncritical belief among the mass of mankind that the preposterous claims of Astrology to be regarded as a valid branch of science had been at last conceded. But in the natural anxiety of scientists to prevent this, they are in danger of throwing out the baby with the bath-water. Astrology as a 'Science' is crammed with easily disprovable assertions. But its origin, which is as old as man himself, arose out of the ineradicable human intuition that man is related in some way to the universe surrounding him, and that life is somehow involved with and dependent on cosmic rhythms. As Michel Ganguelin suggests, 'it would be presumptuous to insist that man never gained a glimpse of the truth in six thousand years of astrological investigations.' It is this kernel of truth that must be recovered and honoured, however shattering it may be to current convictions.

But a grudging acceptance of all these recent researches into rhythms is not enough. We need to open freely our hearts and minds to the astonishing fact of our own total involvement, together with all that lives, in rhythmical processes. Not only all that lives: the rule of rhythm extends to non-living as indisputably as to living matter. Form itself, inorganic as well as organic, is created by the imprint of rhythm on matter. The rhythmic patterns for example, assumed by flowing water when disturbed, its whorls and vortices and sinuous curves, are reproduced with amazing fidelity in the shapes of many marine creatures. To pursue this aspect would take us too far afield, but those who are interested will find it explored with scholarly precision in a fascinating and finely illustrated book called *Sensitive Chaos,* by Theodor Schwenk. Meanwhile we can note in passing the curiously recurrent periodicities of sound, of colour and of atomic weights. And in the field of physical vibrations Dr. Hans Jenny has devised this technique whereby rhythmic vibrations, including those of music and of the human voice, are made visible and then filmed. To see that colour-film is to become aware of a whole new world, as strange and beautiful and disturbing as that other world which was suddenly revealed to us, long ago, by the microscope.

So far we have been glancing at the physical background to the study of rhythm — with the sole aim of establishing its central importance and its universality. This approach of necessity treats rhythm as something seen from the outside, as an objective phenomenon. We are now going to take a journey into the world of rhythm considered as a subjective experience.

*   *   *

Of all human rhythms the most basic are the rhythms of the breathing, and of the beating heart. Heart-muscle is perhaps the most remarkable kind of living tissue that exists. Somewhere within the structure of each individual fibre, independent of any impulses arising from elsewhere, is contained a mysterious power to contract and relax in a self-generated rhythm. This still unexplained power of heart-muscle arises from an unknown source. It must be a source that is close to the origin of life.

And the heart itself, as a functioning whole, is equally close to life's origin. When you listen to another's heart-beats — to the muffled sound of the opening and shutting of miniscule doors in the hidden chambers of the heart — you are in truth eavesdropping, innocently enough, on the top secret of the physical universe. For the heart's alternation of systole-diastole, expulsion-dilation, giving-receiving is the rhythm to which all creation dances.

St. Paul insists that 'the whole creation groaneth'. True, but it also dances. The rhythm of the beating heart is a basic movement in Nature. To be alive to this movement in all its variations is to catch, like a skilled musician, the unifying motif that underlies the magnificent symphony of organic life. It has an immeasurable range, of which it may one day appear that the beating heart of man himself is the mid-point, thus relating him symmetrically to all that lies above and below the man-sized scale: from the microscopic pulsing heart-tube of an ephemerid to the unimaginable rhythm of a cosmic heart, whose systoles and diastoles extend through thousands of millions of terrestrial years.

The concept of a cosmic pulsation may seem pure phantasy. Yet it is curiously in line with contemporary scientific thought. The radio-telescopes of Mount Wilson and Palomar, aided by observations taken from rockets in the vicinity of Mars, are now inclining astronomers to the belief that the principle sustaining the cosmos may perhaps best be represented as the beating of a giant heart. The image that modern astronomy projects is of a huge primordial fireball — compressed to a fantastic degree of density and heat — suddenly exploding into millions of fragments that fly off in all directions to form the innumerable galaxies of the cosmos; these fragments thereafter slowing down through the operation of inter-galactic gravity, and finally reversing their movement and streaming back to re-form the dense flaming fireball from which they sprang; a cycle endlessly repeated.

This fire-ball's degree of density is almost unimaginable by human standards, and sounds rather like science fiction; but it is more than that. Objects called *Pulsars* have recently been discovered in outer space. The density of these Pulsars is such that a teaspoonful of their substance weighs many millions of tons. My authority for this statement is Sir Bernard Lovell, Director of Jodrell Bank.

Even the periodicity of the primordial fire-ball's pulsation has already been calculated, as being of the order of a hundred thousand million years. As yet this is no more than a fashionable scientific hypothesis. But work is being done which may soon yield a higher degree of probability. And if indeed the entire cosmos can be pictured as a gigantic beating heart, a question of ultimate audacity begins at once to rise above the mind's horizon . . . *Whose heart?*

Orthodox religion, of course, has a confident answer: the cosmic systole-diastole, it would claim, is the beating of the heart of God. Which, whatever it may mean, could be true. But a stranger possibility exists, though perhaps in the last analysis it is the same answer in different terms. Now that man has learned to travel through outer space at previously unimaginable speeds, the relativity of human concepts of Time has become obvious. When eventually he achieves, as well he may, speeds approaching the velocity of light, the astronaut will have literally escaped from human time. As Einstein has shown, the interval between his heart-beats, to himself as brief as ever, will measure thousands of terrestrial years. The whole history of our world will be for him compressed into 'one flashing moment of extended time'. Man, crushed and silenced by the immensity of the cosmos in one sense, in another sense may be capable of containing it.

*　　*　　*

The rhythm of the heart-beat belongs to the physical universe. So much so that even the movements of engines are based on the reciprocating pattern of the beating heart. But there is another human rhythm whose affinities lie closer to the inner than the outer world. A man may listen to his own heart-beat, take his own pulse, without affecting its action. It is an objective phenomenon which continues unaltered whether he pays attention to it or not — unless he is an exceptionally nervous soul.

But let him try to listen to his own breathing, and immediately the pattern changes. The rhythm of breathing remains smooth and regular only so long as it remains unconscious. The rhythm of breathing is by this one fact indissolubly connected with the inner world. There are many indications of this. Linguistically the connection is explicit: the Latin *spiritus* means both 'spirit' and 'breath', as does the Greek *pneuma,* and the Hebrew *ruah.* In Christian theology the Third Person of the Trinity is a Spirit and thus, in a literal sense, the Breath of God. To draw breath is the first act of the new-born child. And from then on, in every sense, *inspiring* is connected with life, *expiring* with death. Of all metaphysical disciplines Jnana Yoga is the most clearly aware of this psychic quality in respiration, and its preliminary techniques are closely concerned with the manipulation of breathing.

But the psyche extends infinitely beyond the range of the individual. The psyche also as it were 'breathes' on the historic plane, in slow, centuries-long respirations, inwards to the Centre in the ages of Faith, outward to the external world in the ages of Reason. For the last three hundred years Western man in his passionate predilection for the outward movement has grossly undervalued the equally vital introverted flow of mediaeval feeling. He called it the Dark Age, and regarded it as an unfortunate hiatus in the outward march of the human spirit. A fatal error, for which at last he is showing signs of repentance. In the twentieth century have appeared the first beginnings of a movement in reverse. Psyche is returning to us again out of the ocean of the unconscious, as once Aphrodite was carried to Cytherea on the returning tide. Through the influence of depth psychology Western man begins again to understand and value the dark — that fruitful phase when the outer world loses for a time its overwhelming fascination, when all external things are seen as images, as servants of the invisible, and their secret meaning flows back towards the Centre, refilling the dry cisterns of the soul. But this movement, too, must not be over-valued. To preserve his psychic balance something central in man must 'relax and uncurl and flow as easily as seaweed' with these two great alternating rhythms of extraversion and introversion, giving each in turn its full measure of acceptance.

It should be possible. For the truth is we are rhythmical creatures swimming in a rhythmical ocean of Being. Till now we have never guessed how completely we are surrounded and supported and inter-penetrated in every organ and every separate cell of our bodies by this transcendent force. If we relax, even for a moment, we become aware that the movement of our labouring heart is one with all the intricately interwoven rhythms of Nature. In the same way the rhythm of our mental life is, like breathing, an invisible to-and-fro traffic of giving and taking, losing and re-finding.

For the history of the human mind is not a simple progress story from bewildered ape-man to enlightened modern. The history of the human mind is not a history at all. Religious belief, for example, on which more thought has been expended by man than on any other single subject, has passed apparently through many stages of development; yet Mircea Eliade ended his famous book 'Patterns in Comparative Religion' with this sentence: 'The history of religion can thus, in the last analysis, be expressed in terms of the continual losing and re-finding of religious values, a loss and re-discovery which are never, nor can ever be, final'. The same is true in every field of human thought. What is presented is not a history but rather, to use a term of contemporary art, the kinetic spectacle of a not very large number of primary ideas in constant motion, swaying like pendula through the centuries, first to one extreme then to its opposite, each at its own individual rhythm. To the ear attuned to it there is a kind of music in their motion, always the same, always new, like an infinitely modulated carillon of bells . . .

To return to individual experience, there are, then, two basic rhythms in man — his heart-beat and his breathing. By the one he is related to the whole of organic life, by the other to the life of the spirit. He also carries within himself, as we have seen, innumerable other rhythms, from the flickering alternations within each cell to the slow cyclic recurrences of the periodic diseases. And all this inner awareness of time, all these miraculously synchronising systems have their counterpart at least to some degree in every species of living creature . . . Is it not possible that once fully aware that his inner rhythms are also universal, a man might actually *experience himself* differently, might shed the sick feeling of alienation and find himself at home again in the world?

One fact, at least, is certain: the inconceivable range of the rhythms in which individual consciousness, under certain conditions, can share. This alone is a breakthrough of the hitherto accepted limits of consciousness. It may contain the seeds of a desperately needed psychic mutation.

*   *   *

But even if all this were true — what is the relevance of it to the present world-crisis? It is open to anyone to say that there is none. And I would agree to the extent that I would not advise anybody to step out into the cross-fire of civil war today, armed only with these ideas.

Nevertheless, even the discords of violence have their counterpoint. Hidden in the furious heart of every protester there is a *temenos,* a magic circle of quietness. Held captive here, like Merlin in the enchanted wood, is *puer aeternus,* the immortal child within us, waiting for the word of release. Unfortunately, — or perhaps fortunately — this child within is wide-awake and sharply discriminating. He knows a great deal, this curious child, and cannot be easily deceived. He is only half-convinced by the drop-out paradise of the Singing Heroes, and the clenched-fist world of the Violent Heroes; and is quite unmoved by the sad nostalgic dreams of the traditionalists. He knows that what he waits and listens for is something far different from any of these, something that can never be set up as a New Cause, with frantic partisans; and that if men start raising banners in its support the meaning of it will be already lost. What he is waiting for will come, if it comes at all, silently, 'on dove's feet', into the individual heart. It will be something that is continuously born in beauty, like a fountain in sunlight, out of the endless rhythmic interplay of opposites.

To see life so is to come near to the unstateable meaning of rhythm. It is also to approach the inner significance of what the Nobel Prize physicist Heisenberg has called the Principle of Uncertainty — a new and paradoxical principle on which the whole of modern physics now rests. But far more than physics will eventually rest upon it. To see life so is the key to a world that is for ever open-ended.

That we have temporarily lost our heads in the face of this discovery is painfully obvious. That we may destroy ourselves before we regain our balance is perfectly possible. But there is no way back. The old certainties are dead. It could be the specific achievement of our age not merely to accept this paradoxical quality in life, but to delight in it. Rhythm, which is the cradle of Being, is itself the supreme paradox. It is the never-resting resting-point at the non-existing centre of existence.

Selected References

Chapter I

Copernicus: *see* Arthur Koestler's *The Sleep Walkers* (Hutchinson, 1959)

Levi-Strauss: *Structural Anthropology* (Allen Lane, 1968)

J. Bronowski: *Listener* 21.6.73

John Keats: *The Letters of John Keats* (ed. M. Buxton Forman, 1935)

Gabriel Marcel: quoted by Agnes Arber in *The Manifold and the One* (Murray 1957)

Chapter II

St. Augustine: *Confessions* (Tr.Sheed. Sheed and Ward, 1943)

A.N. Whitehead: *Science and the Modern World* (Cambridge, 1953)

Carlos Castaneda: *Tales of Power* (Simon and Schuster, 1974)

J.W. Krutch: *The Great Chain of Life* (Eyre & Spottiswoode, 1957)

H.W. Lissman: *Electric Location by Fishes* (Scientific American: March 1963)

Lyall Watson: re potatoes and the lunar cycle: *Supernature* (Hodder & Stoughton, 1973)

Cleve Baxter; *Evidence of a Primary Perception in Plant Life* (Int. Journal of Parapsychology 10.4.68)

Ray & Norman Walker: *The Equivocal Principle in Systems Thinking* (General Systems, Vol. XVI 1971)

Chapter III

John Keats: *ibid.*

J.B. Haldane: quoted in *The Times*, 1.5.75

SELECTED REFERENCES

Berthelot: quoted by Panwels & Bergier in *The Dawn of Magic* (Panther Books, 1967).

Brunetiere: *ibid.*

Lippman: *ibid.*

Moissan: *ibid.*

Teilhard de Chardin: *The Phenomenon of Man* (Collins, 1959)

Jacques Monod: *Chance and Necessity* (New York & London, 1971)

Heinrich Helmholtz: quoted by Rosalind Heywood in *The Sixth Sense* (London, 1959)

Arthur Koestler: *The Case of the Midwife Toad* (Hutchinson, 1971)

Chapter V

Anthony Huxley: *Plant and Planet* (Allen Lane, 1974)

Chapter VI

Johan Huizinga: *Homo Ludens* (M.T. Smith, 1970)

Chapter VIII

Preston Harold: *The Shining Stranger* (Wayfarer Press, New York, 1967)

J. Genet: *The Thief's Journal* (Faber, 1973)

C.G. Jung: *Psychological Reflections* (Routledge & Kegan Paul, 1963)

R.D. Laing: *The Divided Self* (Tavistock Publications, 1960)

Chapter IX

John Livingstone Lowes: *The Road to Xanadu* (Houghton Mifflin, 1927)

C.G. Jung: *Memories, Dreams, Reflections* (Collins, Routledge & Paul, 1963)

Morton Kelsey: *Dreams, the Dark Speech of the Spirit* (Doubleday, 1968)

Rainer Maria Rilke: *The Duino Elegies* (Hogarth Press, 1939)

Chapter X

Maeterlinck: *The Life of the Ant* (Cassell & Co., 1930)

Chapter XI

Richard Noone: *In Search of the Dream People* (W. Morrow 1972)

Ronald Siegal: re the Umgana Tree: quoted by *Anthony Huxley*, ibid. p. 283.

Chapter XII

F. Kummel: *On the Concept of Time* (1962)

E. Kant: quoted in *The Voices of Time* (ed. J. Fraser; Allen Lane Penguin Press, 1968)

Chapter XIII

St. Luke: 1.46-53

C. Nodier: quoted by L.L. Whyte in *The Unconscious before Freud* (Tavistock Pub., 1962)

H.F. Amiel: *Journal Intime* (Tr. Mrs. Humphrey Ward. MacMillan, 1909)

Morton Kelsey: *ibid.*

Chapter XV

Novalis: *Hymns to the Night* (Phoenix Press, 1948)

Hans Jenny: *Cymatics* (Basileus Press, Basel, 1967)

Preston Harold: *ibid.*

Theodore Schwenck: *Sensitive Chaos* (R. Steiner Press, 1965)